Why My Son?

• • •

Sue D'Ambrosio

. . .

Acknowledgements

I would first like to thank my husband, Pasquale, and daughter, Karla, for their patience and support while I wrote this book. Both sides of our family have been so supportive, but I'd like to say a special thanks to my five siblings- Carol, Sandy, Mary, John, and Joe- I will forever be grateful to you all for loving my son so much and always being a special part of his life as he was growing up. And last, but not least, I need to thank my beautiful mother and father who have always been there for me, have loved their grandson unconditionally throughout his life, and have lent their support whenever I needed it as writing this book about my son was a true emotional ride and one that I never thought I would have been challenged with in life.

•••

Introduction

This is a powerful story of how the beautiful life of my son, Mark, spiraled out of control. His life was taken by the disease of drug addiction on February 12, 2010, at the age of nineteen. This story teaches us about how addiction is not a choice; it is a disease. It seriously affects all the loved ones of the person who is addicted; however, the one suffering the most is the person who has the disease and does not know how to overcome it, especially at a young age.

Through my personal conversations with my son, I can tell you he struggled continually for years, but he was always trying to move forward in a positive way, just like many people who have an addiction.

Mark had so many people that loved him. He will always hold a huge place inside of our hearts. We love him and miss him very much and hope that some good will come out of this story to help someone who may be struggling.

•••

Chapter One

The old saying is that your children are a reflection of you. That may be true in general but not when it comes to the disease of drug addiction. When someone becomes addicted, he or she takes on a new personality. Addicts lie, steal, cheat, or do whatever it takes to get what they need—drugs! It happened to my son, Mark, and if you're a parent who thinks that it could never happen to your child, you might need to change how you think.

Mark was born on September 5, 1990. He was such a beautiful baby. At twenty-two, I was excited to be a new mom. My then husband and I had been living in New Jersey, and having Mark was a true blessing, not only for us, but for our families too. Although Mark's father and I had our issues, we both enjoyed being parents, and we were so proud of this kid. He was a happy child, always pleasant with everyone.

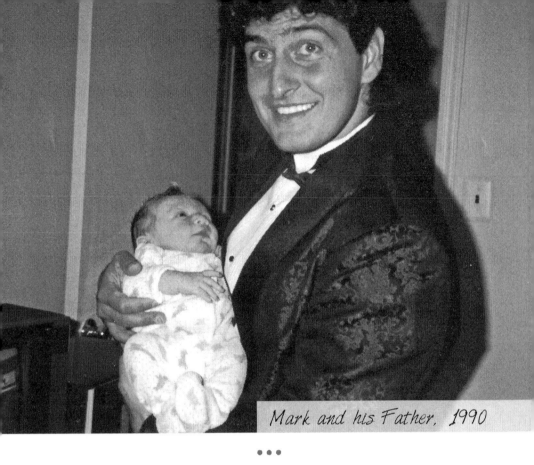

Mark and his Father, 1990

...

Mark and I in our first home, 1990

We moved around a lot when Mark was one and two and finally decided to stay put in South Jersey when he was three. We had lived in many places, including Florida and the Jersey Shore. As we started growing as a family, Mark's father and I were not growing as a couple, so we separated for a few months when Mark was three. It became a little traumatic for him; he missed his father when he wasn't around. We decided to try to see if the relationship could be saved by being apart for a little while so we both could sort out what we wanted for the future. After a few months, we decided to try again and see what would happen once we were all living under the same roof again. Mark was happy having his mom and dad back together again, but it was short lived. We soon decided, in part due to advice from my counselor, that we were better off being apart than together, as we were both unhappy.

My husband and I separated as Mark was turning four. My son and I moved into a new place. It was an amicable separation, but it wasn't an easy transition. Now I was a single parent of a four-year-old. I held two jobs, and for a short time I worked three jobs so I could afford the place where I was living. It was an adjustment I had to embrace.

The arrangements regarding Mark were that he would be living with me, and his father would take him every other weekend and one day during the week for a couple of hours. I don't know if it was the best situation, but we were getting used to the schedule.

Wanting to just put this whole situation behind me, I filed for divorce in December of 1994, and our divorce was finalized in June of 1995. All that was on my mind at the time was that I wanted my son to be okay with all of this. I was determined to make his life as normal as possible under the circumstances.

On the weekends he was with me, we were out and about. We went to all kinds of festivals and day trips, and we went to all the fun things going on in our town; you name it, and we were out. We went out so often and did so many fun things that Mark would always ask me, "So where are we going next?" I decided we were going to make the best of our situation. I come from a big family with two brothers and three sisters, and I wanted Mark to have all of the great experiences that we had as a close family. Being a single parent was no easy task, but I knew I would have some help, as my whole family was there for me and loved Mark so much. They were very involved in his life as he was growing up. He was the only grandchild at the time, and he really became the light of our family.

As it became a routine thing for Mark to go back and forth for visitation, it must have been tough to not have his mom and dad together. Sometimes he told me that when he was with his dad he missed me, and when he was with me he missed his dad. I tried not to feed into it too much because things were never going to be the same as it was, and this was something that we just had to get used to.

So life went on, and I met my husband, Pasquale, when Mark was four and a half years old, a month before my divorce was final. We hit it off right away, but I was not ready to get my son involved until I got to know Pasquale first. As he and I got to know each other, we started to do things that included Mark too, and everything seemed to be going pretty well. We dated a year and got engaged, and then we married fifteen months later. Now, by age seven, Mark was adjusting to a new dad in the house. Everything was going okay, and when Mark was a little over eight years old, we had our daughter, Karla. Mark's father had been in a relationship also, and he remarried a few years after Pasquale and I did.

Everything seemed to be going pretty well; Mark was still going to his father's every other weekend like usual, and my husband and I were having fun being the parents of two children and didn't start noticing too much of a change with Mark at this point. Along with my new marriage came a whole new family with cousins for Mark. He had some great times with his two favorite cousins.

It had been a gradual thing, but I think the more Mark saw my husband and spent time with him, the harder it was for him when he went to his father's. I started to sense he may have been struggling with who he was going to like better. I had told him when I got remarried that he could love both his dad and his stepdad. He didn't have to choose; he could have a great relationship with both of them. Mark used to say after I remarried that he was happy as long as I was happy, and he felt the same about his dad, and I believed him.

• • •

Mark and my husband, Pasquale, 1995

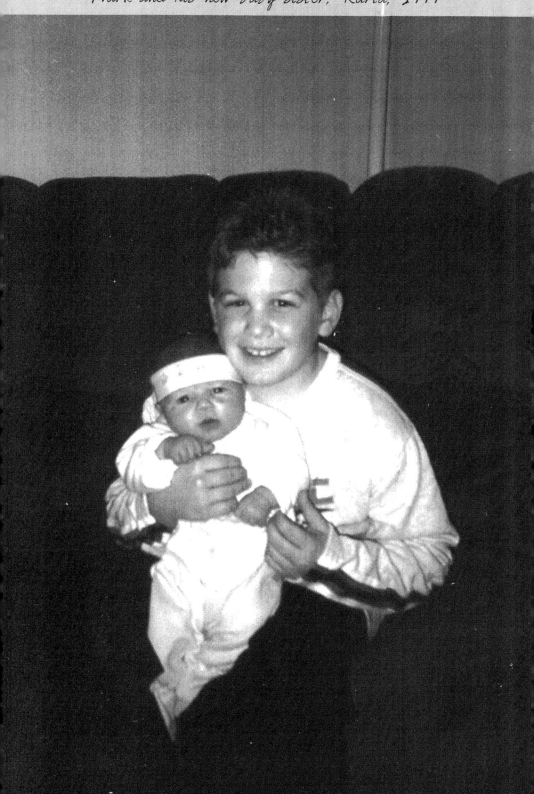

Mark and his new baby sister, Karla, 1999

Mark and Karla on our first family vacation, Hershey, PA, summer of 1999

• • •

Looking back on this, I'm not sure if Mark was really fine with all of these changes. I think it may have gotten a little confusing for him at times; he may not have known how to feel as he was getting close to my husband yet was still close to his father. I think he started to react to the situation, and he gave his father a hard time when he was picking him up for weekend visitation. Mark's father became concerned and decided to take him to a counselor, and gradually things started to get back on track.

Mark was in elementary school when he was going through all of this, and although at times he needed to work on self-control, he was a smart kid and had terrific grades, always making honor roll. He was one of the lucky ones, always absorbed in class and could do really well without having to study too much. He was also well liked and always had a lot of friends.

One day I ran into a parent whose child went to school with Mark, and she mentioned that she thought Mark was such a great kid. She said he was the only one who would strike up a conversation with them, and they would barely get a hello out of any of the other kids that came to their home. That was my Mark. The family used to call him the politician, and he was.

While Mark was in nursery school and elementary school, one of the things I liked the most was being a room parent, where you would come to your child's classroom and help out with the parties they had throughout the year. Every year I'd volunteer for the parties and other events. The day that I was helping out with his fourth-grade party, his teacher and I were talking. I asked her how he was doing besides being a good student, and she said something that I have never forgotten. She said she worried that he was a follower, and she couldn't have been more right.

Chapter Two

Mark's self-destruction didn't start until halfway through middle school. Because four local elementary schools in the area were combined to form the middle school, Mark met some new kids in sixth grade. Some of the kids he knew already from playing baseball for our township. The league included kids from all four elementary schools in the township; Mark started playing T-ball for one year and then baseball after that every year. He also played roller hockey for a few years, too, but I knew baseball was his passion. He liked competing and being part of a team, and we liked going to the games. It really kept him busy all the time.

His school year started out great; we received a notice in the mail that Mark was a participant in a talent search conducted by The Johns Hopkins University Center for Talented Youth for the year 2001 for mathematics and verbal skills. We were so happy and knew that he had a lot of potential to do great things in the future as long as he kept up with his academics.

As he got adjusted to middle school, Mark started to hang around a new group of kids and took up a new hobby, skateboarding. We didn't have any problem with it, and we took him to the skate parks that he and his friend liked to go to. In the beginning we would meet other families to talk while Mark skated, but as Mark entered the seventh and eighth grade, he wanted to go by himself with his friends more. I was upset that he wanted to be with me less, but I was told by another mom that at this age they stray a little, so we began giving him a little more freedom. His skateboarding group was now hanging out more and more, which meant there was more pressure on my husband and me to allow him to sleep over at friends' houses more, which they were starting to do. I wasn't too happy with some of the newfound friends, and we told Mark that we didn't care for the new attitude he had. His personality started changing, and it was really upsetting to see this change in him. We brought up the fact that we noticed he was acting too wild and crazy when he was around certain friends, always trying to imitate what they were doing, and we couldn't stand that. We learned many years later that he and some of his friends walked to an elementary school nearby and jumped off the roof of the building. None of the parents knew at the time they were doing this. We also didn't know that they were unsupervised pretty much all the time from what Mark later told me. I wish I had known this was going on.

My ex-husband and I agree that we did not share the same views on who Mark should be hanging out with. I had told Mark's father it was a constant battle all the time, and Mark would bring up the fact that his father was fine with his friends, and we should be too. My husband and I talked about how Mark would be a little too wild when he was with his friends, and we didn't like it one bit. His father said he did not feel as strongly about it as my husband and I did but asked us why we allowed sleepovers at these friends' houses since we didn't approve of them, and our answer was that we really got tired of the constant fighting. It was a no-win situation and too stressful to try to convince Mark on our own that we didn't want him spending so much time with these friends and being away from our home. There wasn't too much we could do about it, as the friendships were already established. The more we argued about it, the more he wanted to rebel. Because of all this, I knew that I was going to watch him with his friends more closely now. We could not control what went on the weekends we were not with him, but we tried our best when he was with us.

Saddened that Mark didn't understand how my husband and I felt was making me stressed out. Whenever I would mention different things that I didn't like, Mark would disagree with me, and I told him that I was going to continue to call things as I saw them, and it was too bad if he didn't like what I said; I was his mom. Because of the conflicts we had at home I had Mark talk to a counselor at school during this time, but I knew that we were not going to change his mind about the friends, so we began having them over more to get to know them better.

Mark was playing baseball for the township and still doing well in school, so I tried to ease up on him a little. I didn't want our relationship to always be full of negativity now. One of the things I have always loved about Mark is that he would always say something to make me laugh. If I was having a bad day, I could always count on Mark to cheer me up. We had always had fun with him, and he was a preteen, so I knew we were going to expect some attitude. It was all part of the growing up stage; what parent hasn't dealt with some attitude?

Chapter Three

It was the start of seventh grade, and Mark still was spending a lot of time with his friends, not wanting to go where we were going as a family at times when things would come up, and again the arguments started. Mark's dad and my husband both worked two jobs, which left little time for them to spend time with Mark one on one as he got older. Angrily, I had told both of the dads before that I could not be both a mom and a dad to Mark. They both knew how I felt about it, and I said I was tired of hearing that he wanted to be with his friends and didn't want to hang out, because I think it was just the opposite. I think Mark was angry, and he was unable to express how he felt at the time.

It was middle school graduation time, and because of his outstanding grades, Mark received a President's Award for academic excellence. We were really proud of him and knew he was a terrific student. I guess we figured whatever was going on with him was just a teenager thing, and everything would get better.

But there would be more challenges ahead as Mark entered high school. After freshman year of high school, he decided he had enough of baseball. A lot of the friends he was hanging out with were quitting at that time. Being a follower, he wanted to do the same. We knew he loved this sport, so we tried to convince him, his coach tried to convince him, and even his teammates tried to convince him, but he had made up his mind. I was really sad about that decision because I knew he had always loved the sport and was good at it. There was a tournament team forming for the summer, and I tried to convince him that he should go for it. I also knew that having too much time on your hands equals trouble, and that was exactly what I was trying to avoid. Mark said he would try to get involved in other activities in his high school when school started, so even though I was sad that we would not get to watch his baseball games anymore, my husband and I supported his decision. There was no way we were going to force him to play if he did not want to anymore.

• • •

Mark and Karla, early high school years, summer 2005

It was midsummer now, right before Mark's sophomore year of high school, and I wish I had known at the time what he was getting himself into. He was only fourteen years old. The group he was hanging out with began to smoke marijuana. He told me they were all hanging out one day, and he and one of his friends were offered a joint to smoke for the first time. He said at first he did not want to try it—he was going to walk away—but later he gave in, maybe due to peer pressure, and he ended up liking it.

My husband and I had spoken about drugs many times with Mark, and from the time he was little he had said he would never do drugs. He had been through all the drug awareness programs in elementary and middle school, and we were confident that he got the message about what to do if he was ever around anyone who did drugs. Even when we were around my family, we used to laugh and say how cute he was with how seriously he said he would never do drugs. So it was that much more unexpected for us when we were told at a later time that he actually was using drugs.

We did not know what was going on so there was no suspicion on our part as to any drug use going on in the group at this time, and I didn't hear about anyone from his school getting in trouble with drugs. When I look back on when Mark was this age, I didn't feel there was a need to worry about drugs being an issue even when we went through some rough times with him when he was in middle school. Kids go through so many changes all the time, especially when they are in the middle school and high school years. We had hoped that setting good values at home through the years would have made him a strong enough person to walk away when he was first offered drugs. But that moment when he changed his mind and decided for whatever reason to try that drug forever changed his life and ours.

It was the beginning of his sophomore year, and Mark and a group of his friends, both guys and girls, decided to go into a video store that would be closing for good soon. A mom of one of the girls in this group was working there at the time. Someone in the group decided to go in the back room where the X-rated videos were. Mark had a backpack ready while one of the kids grabbed a video off the shelf and put it in the backpack. They were caught right away by the owner of the store, and he told the girl's mom who worked there that he was going to prosecute Mark and his friend or all of the teenagers that were there. The mom convinced the owner not to prosecute. She asked him if they could help her hand out some flyers to the surrounding neighborhoods that would help him, due to the fact that his store would be closing soon, which could act as their punishment, and he agreed. I got the call after it happened and was totally shocked. I had to ask my son why he would do such a thing. He didn't have an answer for me. One of the girls in the group said that it wasn't Mark's fault, and I told Mark I didn't care whose idea it was to do this; it was wrong, and he knew it. We grounded him as his punishment.

● ● ●

Chapter Four

The weeks flew by, and a friend of Mark's was having people over to his house for his birthday party. We had known
the parents since our kids were little, and Mark, by now,
was off punishment. The plan was that Mark would go to
the party and spend the night at the house of one of his
friends after the party. Someone had brought alcohol with
them, and when they left the party, Mark and a couple of
his buddies started drinking as they were walking back to
the house where they were spending the night. I was told
that as they were in the neighborhood of the friend they
were going to spend the night at, a neighbor noticed them
staggering and being loud and alerted the friend's father.
He came out to check it out and saw that they were drunk.
Mark didn't look good to him, so he decided to call the
cops to see if Mark could be brought to the hospital to be
checked out.

We got a call in the wee hours of the morning from a
cop saying that Mark was in our local hospital for alcohol

poisoning and was already in a room. I started getting upset, and I rushed over and met one of the police officers at the hospital. He took me to the floor where Mark was, and a nurse showed me to his room. The nurse took his vital signs, and when we heard him moaning, she smirked a little bit. She told me she had a son who went through the same thing with alcohol. I was relieved that Mark was going to be okay but upset at the same time. His alcohol test showed moderately severe alcohol poisoning, but I was planning on telling him that his levels were so high he was lucky to be alive so he would come to his senses. He was in no shape to come home right away, so they moved an extra bed next to his, and I was able to sleep there for a few hours. When he finally woke up, I just looked at him, shaking my head in disbelief. I kept thinking how crazy this all was and what we as parents were going to do about it.

I was finally able to take him home in the morning, and all I kept hearing was a million apologies from Mark. When we arrived home, my husband and I talked to Mark about what had happened. We told him he had better get his act together. He could tell we were obviously emotional about what had happened, but the main thing we concentrated on was that he was going to be okay. We did not see the signs of drug use, which was already going on, because he hid it very well. We were firm with how we wanted things to start changing with him, and we hoped our talk about the trouble he was getting into was sinking in. We punished him, but we wanted more than his word that he would straighten up. We wanted to see that he was changing by his actions, like hanging around the right influences and staying out of trouble. I don't think Mark realized at the time what he was getting himself into, and we had no idea what was going on either. Why would we as parents see the signs anyway? We did not use drugs.

As the weeks went by, Mark branched off a bit with a friend who I thought was not part of this group. I had never seen this kid before; he seemed nice and looked clean cut to us, and we were happy about that because it meant that Mark would be around more. Mark decided to finally have his hair cut short, like his friend, after keeping it long for a few years. With the new look and some weight loss from my husband and I helping him change his diet, Mark looked like a totally different kid now. My husband and I were happy with how things were going, and there was finally peace at home.

•••

Chapter Five

One Saturday, my sister and I decided to go shopping. Mark didn't feel like going along, so I just took my daughter with me and left him and his friend at the house. As we were out shopping, I got a call from my husband that there was something he needed to tell me. He said Mark was smoking marijuana. He said he had been looking for something in the drawer in our kitchen and found a small bag of pot. I asked him what drawer he had found it in, and when he told me, I began to laugh. I told him it was catnip I was filling up one of the cat toys with the other day, and I threw the bag in there while straightening up. I later told Mark about it and, not knowing that he had already tried marijuana, we both laughed about it.

Tryouts for baseball for the high school team had come; Mark knew it was competitive, and he tried out but did not make the team. Mark became discouraged so I told him to look into getting involved in other activities he might like at the school. After a couple months went by, my husband had had enough and said if Mark was not going to find something to get involved with at school, he needed to look for a job. All I kept thinking about was the Italian deli my husband had owned for a period of eleven years in the past. This would have been the perfect job for Mark if it hadn't been sold when he was twelve. I didn't know who would hire a fifteen-year-old but mentioned to Mark that he needed to start looking for a job.

Mark had been watching his weight, and I thought it was a good idea that he had joined a nearby gym with a couple of friends. One day when they were all working out, they ran into someone they knew who mentioned a restaurant that would hire them. I got a call from Mark later that day with what I thought was good news. He said that I was going to be really proud of him and that he had already had an interview at a local restaurant and got the job, and so did his friends. My husband and I were so happy that he got a job and was starting right away. We were really relieved because it meant a lot of his after-school time he would be working, and that meant staying out of trouble, so we thought this was a step in the right direction. The excitement didn't last long though. After a couple of months he was getting tired of having to work what he called "lousy hours" and a lot of weekend shifts he was getting, so he quit.

We were really counting on him staying with the job for a while. His boredom from not keeping busy with after-school activities was worrying me again now that he wasn't even working. We were not aware, though, that Mark had gotten himself a new job—selling marijuana. He was given an offer to deal drugs by one of his buddies, so he got his first scale and began to sell. We were not aware what was up, but I noticed that when he was at home, he was always going outside on his cell phone. I thought it was strange and brought it up to my husband that Mark was on his cell too much, always going outside so we couldn't hear his conversations. He asked me what I thought Mark was doing, and I didn't have a clue. He told me he didn't think Mark was up to anything and said it was a teenager thing, and I should let it go. Despite everything that had happened so far, we had a great family, and we still did not suspect Mark could be using or selling drugs. Would anyone think that their own child would ever do something like this?

Mark called me one day and asked if his friend could stay for dinner, and I said yes. They both came home, and Mark's friend told him that they should go upstairs and wash their hands before they eat. They were being overly nice to me, and I started getting a little suspicious. After they ate and said they were going to go out for a little bit, I got curious. I don't know what made me do it—maybe it was a mother's instinct—but I decided to go up to his room and look in his nightstand, in his chest of drawers, and under his bed—nothing. Then I stared at his book bag. I opened it up, and tucked in a small compartment I found a bag of marijuana. I started getting upset and called him up right away. When I told him what I had just found, he said he was holding it for his friend and it wasn't his. I told him it was already gone, so he wouldn't be giving it to any friend. I told my husband what had happened. As far as we knew, Mark hadn't tried marijuana before. Mark denied it, his friend said it was his, and we told Mark to come clean about if he had tried it. Of course he told me he had not. I didn't want to believe that this was really happening. I told Mark that people who used drugs are not the right kind of people to be hanging out with. My husband and I were upset, and we called Mark's father about it. My husband and I sat down with Mark and discussed the issue and let him know how we felt about it. I needed a little time to let this all sink in, though. I don't think any of us knew how to handle Mark at that point.

Within a matter of days, I got a call from the police to come pick Mark up at the police station. The officer told me two of the kids that were with Mark were arrested for possession of marijuana. Mark was not arrested because he was not physically seen smoking it, and no charges would be filed. On the ride home, I told Mark, "It shouldn't really surprise me what has happened because you have been hanging out with kids that are a bunch of troublemakers."

My husband became really disappointed in Mark and started distancing himself from him. My husband believed Mark just wasn't listening to anyone but his friends and was doing stupid things. Little did we know that he had an addiction to marijuana and was trying other drugs too. We did not see any signs in the beginning, and Mark must have hidden his addiction really well. My husband and I do not do drugs, so we did not have the experience in how to deal with Mark's behavior. I did not learn much about addiction until a few years ago. I have a better understanding now of what it really is, a true disease.

...

Chapter Six

Considering how things were going, I decided to go up to Mark's high school to let the vice principal know that I needed to do something about what was going on with Mark. He was cutting the occasional class, which we found out because a note was sent home about it. Mark also started missing school sometimes, so I was reaching out for help. It wasn't Mark's personality to be this way, and the vice principal referred me to the school counselor, so I made Mark go see her soon afterward. I bought a drug kit at the pharmacy and decided when he came home from school one day that he was going to take the test. I called his Father to come over so we could confront him together. He was a little resistant about taking it, so I knew right then that it would come out positive. He finally took the test, and when it came up positive for marijuana, Mark's father and I were both upset and disappointed. Mark said he wasn't using even though it came up positive.

I told him it was now time to take a little drive somewhere. I had called my sister who knew someone who worked in a police department out of state who suggested I could take him down to this police station for a talk. On the way, Mark kept asking me where we were going, and as we pulled up, I think he was a little scared. I thought they would put a little fear in him so he would straighten up.

When we arrived, an officer there got in Mark's face and talked to him about respecting himself and others. The officer put Mark in a jail cell with someone inside who told him what it was like to be in a jail cell. I think it was scary for him, and I think it made him uneasy being with the guy alone in that cell, which had been a set up. After the officer talked with Mark, we left. I saw how angry Mark was that I had brought him down there, and I knew that it didn't do any good. When we got in the car, I looked at Mark and asked him, "Have I ever told you how much I love you, kid?"

He said, "Mom, you tell me every day."

So I said, "Okay, just checking to make sure you knew that."

I talked the whole way home about all the things that had happened to him so far and let him know we were not going to tolerate his behavior.

To punish him, we shut down his cell phone service. We thought that maybe it would finally sink in that we wanted him to wise up. That plan didn't last too long, though, because we had a hard time tracking him down, especially after school when my husband and I were both working. It started to get really annoying calling Mark's friends up to ask where he was.

Again, he had always been a good student, even taking honors classes, but eventually Mark told us he wanted to drop down to the next level because advanced classes were too much for him. Sometimes he complained about going to school at all, and some of his grades were dropping a little bit, which wasn't like him.

One day when I went to work, I just started crying and told my manager that I was so upset about the way Mark was acting lately. I then called my parents and told them I was sick about what had been going on, and my dad suggested I go to the high school and confront Mark immediately, if I was able to leave work, and he and my mom would meet me there. I also called my husband, and he met us there too. I left a message to let Mark's father know what the plan was. I told the school office to get Mark out of class immediately but not to tell him we were coming to the school.

I let my work know I was leaving and that it was important. All of my co-workers have been so supportive and knew what my situation was, so I knew it was going to be okay to leave for the high school. When I got there, I was shown to the vice principal's office where we all met up with Mark and had a talk. We asked the vice principal to stay while we talked to Mark about what was going on with him. My parents and I were crying at this point, and Mark did not respond to our questions, so we made a decision to take him to the local crisis center to have him checked out. We knew he was on something, and when we got there, he had to be checked in. As he was sitting there, he put his hands in his pocket like he was reaching for something. I made a motion to the security guard. He was going to be tested after checking in, and, at that moment, all I could do was cry, thinking "How did it get this far with him?" He was such a great kid with such potential, and here we were at a crisis center.

They tested Mark for drugs, and he went into a room where they asked him a lot of questions. At this point he only wanted my husband in the room with him because he was angry with me for taking him there. His father had been at a meeting and could not make it to the school or the center. A few hours later, the doctor came out to tell us Mark was not a danger to himself or others, and the only drug he had tested positive for was marijuana. Before we left, they suggested in the future we could call a rehab for outpatient care if we needed to, but most of the outpatient rehabs were for users of stronger drugs like cocaine and heroin.

Mark was still angry with me for bringing him to the crisis center, but I knew at the time it was the right thing to do. I don't think he realized then that we were all trying to help him, not hurt him. I remember Mark telling me that he thought pot was nothing but a plant that you smoke and not a drug. Again, not being addicts or experts in the field of addiction, my husband and I did not realize that Mark already had a really bad addiction.

···

Chapter Seven

As the weeks went by, because I didn't trust Mark, I decided to put my "FBI skills" to the test. When I was growing up, my mother said I was always the one that found anything that was lost. I had a good eye for things, and when Mark was out and I was home, I would check his room. One day when I was searching his room, I flipped up the mattress of his bed and found an envelope from our local hospital. When I opened it, it was the paperwork to fill out to be a volunteer at our local hospital, which I had signed him up for a few months earlier. This was something I had suggested to Mark when all this craziness started, and we talked about him doing some volunteer work. He agreed to let me sign him up at the time, and I thought it would be good for him to do. So there it was, hidden in between the mattresses.

I was so mad that he hadn't turned in the paperwork, but I didn't bring it up to him right away because he would then know I was searching his room, and I wanted to keep on searching. When I brought it up to my husband, I told him I hoped that because of all the lying that had gone on, I hoped Mark wasn't doing anything shady, and I thought that Mark was on that cell phone of his a little too much again. My husband said Mark would never do something like that, not after all that had happened, and I should stop worrying. I decided to call our phone carrier and get a statement sent showing how many text messages were sent and received by Mark's phone. There were 850 text messages in one month.

One day when I was in Mark's room checking again, I saw something under his nightstand that I had never seen. After looking at this machine for a little bit, I wasn't sure what it was. I left it there and decided to keep looking around. I took a look at his closet and stared at his clothes and thought that this would be a good place for someone to hide something. I began looking in every shirt pocket and pants pocket. Sure enough, I found what looked like drug paraphernalia. As crazy as this may sound, I even put a pair of gloves on and went through his whole trash can and found some empty little plastic bags, which turned out to be dime bags used for drug selling. I called Mark, telling him only that I had found a contraption in his room and asked him what it was. Mark said it was for a chemistry project. I asked him if he really thought that I was a fool and wouldn't figure out what it was. But I really wasn't sure yet what the device was, and I simply told him he had better be on his way home.

My husband came home right after I had called Mark. After looking at the contraption I found, he said he thought it was a scale to sell drugs with. We just looked at each other, not saying a word. The anger was building up, and my husband called Mark, screaming, and told him he had better be almost home. Not a minute later, he walked through the door. We were so aggravated and could not even think straight at this point. I called Mark's father, and he was mad too and told us that if Mark wanted to go down this path, then let him get busted. I threw the scale out, but I was not about to look the other way and let things continue this way under my roof. We were not going to sweep this under the rug, and I wasn't about to let my kid fall. Of course we grounded Mark, but the fact that we were a blended family did not help with the disciplining process. My husband said that whenever he stepped in, it made the relationship worse between the two of them. I was tired of doing the disciplining on my own all the time, and it was very stressful. We needed help, and I wanted the four of us, together as parents, to straighten it all out because it was getting out of hand. No good parent is going to allow this in their house, and at this age, kids still need to be guided in the right direction. I looked into finding a counselor and set up an appointment right away. Unfortunately for my son, his insurance would only allow so many visits, but we were going to keep taking him until the visits ran out.

We started meeting with the counselor once a week, and the process got Mark to open up about his feelings. I don't think he liked that the counselor was able to get some things out of him, like the fact that he was upset that he was not able to spend much time with his father. I guess everyone was trying to make a living, and for financial reasons there wasn't much free time available for my ex-husband to spend with Mark doing the father and son thing. His father had joined Mark and I at one of the sessions and agreed that they should spend more time together. I felt better that Mark was expressing how he had been feeling, and I hoped this counselor would be able to address Mark's problems as time went on.

The only thing my son and I fought over at this point was the fact that he continued to see the same friends even though he knew he kept getting into trouble when he was with them. Everything he had done so far would not change the fact that I loved my child so much and would do whatever it took to get him back on track. I was glad that he was expressing his anger, and I thought it could only get better in time. At fifteen years old, I don't think young people have the maturity to really express themselves the right way when they are feeling bad about something. We thought progress would be made with continued counseling.

∙ ∙ ∙

Chapter Eight

As time went by, Mark started to not get up for school, and I decided since I could not physically grab him out of bed in the morning, I would call the school for him. When they asked me why he wasn't coming to school, instead of saying he was sick, I told them it was because he didn't feel like it. After many missed days, I got a surprise call one day. It was the vice principal of his high school. He had noticed that Mark had many absences and asked where Mark was, and I said he was sleeping. He said not to leave for work yet, and he would be there within fifteen minutes. Shocked and not knowing that they did this at the school, I waited for the knock on the door. Accompanying the vice principal was a police officer who worked on-site at the high school. I let them in, and the vice principal walked right up to Mark's bedroom and kicked the bed and told him to get up. I think Mark himself was startled. I guess anyone would be if they were awakened by the vice principal while still wearing their boxers! Mark took his time and then went to their car, not even looking at me as he was leaving. I said good-bye and told him to have a great day.

Before the officer walked out, I confided in her, while crying, that I found a scale and had thrown it out. She said, like I had, that he had been hanging around the wrong crowd and that they came to the house to help because they had known that we had already tried to help him by taking him to the crisis center not too long ago. I told her he had started seeing a counselor, and she told me to let her know how he did as time passed. I thanked her, and they were on their way.

One day after Mark got home from school and I was off from work, he came home and said he was headed to the gym and would be back later. Not thinking anything was going on, I went about doing what I was doing. After all, we were taking him to a counselor, and I didn't think he would be doing shady things anymore. When it was time for dinner he wasn't home, and I called his cell. I got his voice mail and left a message. After dinner he strolled in. I took one look at him and knew something was up, so I asked him where he had been and why didn't he pick up his cell phone. I could tell that his eyes looked a little glassy and confronted him about it. I told him that I thought he had been smoking marijuana instead of being at the gym. Of course, he denied it, but I knew he wasn't telling the truth and decided while he was downstairs that I would go upstairs and call the gym. I asked if they could check their system to see if he had checked into the gym, and they said he did not.

Now he was caught in another lie. I was furious and told my husband about it. He said I was jumping to conclusions and that he didn't think Mark would be doing anything shady again after everything he had gone through and since he was seeing a counselor. He said Mark looked okay to him, and maybe Mark just felt like hanging out and had told me he went to the gym to avoid the questions I would have asked him because of the strained trust between Mark and me. All I kept thinking was that my son wasn't right, this wasn't normal, and things were really changing at home and getting out of control. I wasn't going to let this go.

I frequently asked Mark what was wrong or how I could help him when he got so angry at the littlest things and slammed the cabinets in our house. It was so strange that he was acting this way, and I thought it could not just be from smoking marijuana. My parents said they observed in Mark someone who was becoming withdrawn and distant when they babysat my daughter once a week. Being a retired family physician, my father said that he thought that Mark might be taking some pills, as he seemed irritated a lot of the time and that marijuana wouldn't make a person act like that. He suggested that I take Mark to see his family doctor, so I set up an appointment. When it was time to go to the appointment, Mark was giving me a hard time about it, but I managed to get him there anyway.

The doctor started checking him and had a talk about his drug use. He was given a prescription to go to the lab to get tested, and, of course, he complained about it and walked away instead of getting in the car. All I kept think-ing about was that I was really getting tortured. Just as I was about to leave the parking lot to go after him, I got a call from Mark saying he would take the test now if I picked him up. It came up positive for marijuana but not for pills. I was told it may have been out of his system already. At the suggestion of the doctor we continued to monitor Mark's behavior and began reading on the internet about the symptoms a person has while under the influence of differ-ent drugs.

One day Mark and his friend were at our house. They were planning a night out with some people. Mark knew what his curfew was, and when they both left, I didn't sus-pect that anything unusual was going on. Even though we sometimes took things away as punishment and restricted him from going out, we got opinions from family who said that we should keep him in on the weekends for a while.

Both my husband and I had fallen asleep early that night. In the middle of the night, we got a knock on our door. It was the police, looking for Mark. There had been an incident at a big party that Mark and his friends were at, and one of Mark's friends had been kicked in the head and was in the hospital. The officers wanted to make sure Mark and the friends he was with were okay. I remember getting really uptight about it because Mark wasn't home yet, and they asked if I had any of the addresses of the kids I thought he might be with so they could speak with the other par-ents. I took a guess as to who he might be with, and they were able to alert all the parents of the kids that were with Mark. The police eventually found Mark and his friends safe and dropped Mark off at our house. I was so glad that he was fine, but I was annoyed that a kid who was older than Mark had had a party when his parents were out of town and had been arrested.

A few days later, I got a call from the father of the kid who had the party. He had also called other parents. He said his house was completely ransacked and things were stolen. He was so upset. His son had told him that he had a bunch of kids over, and when Mark overheard the conversation, he said, "Mom, the whole school was there!" The dad was trying to play the blame game, saying my son and another kid were calling people to come over. I told the father that his son was the one that had the party, and I really wanted to say that no one had a gun to his kid's head to have it. I told him I was very sorry that he was in this situation, but he should not have left a teenager home alone knowing he could possibly have a party.

The father said that Mark and some other kids had damaged a car of his and that there were some cigarette holes in the back of the seats, so he asked for money from us to repair it because his son told him the names of the kids that had done it. He said none of the other parents of the other kids gave him a dime. He asked if we could send some money to him and be generous about it. We sat Mark down and told him about the conversation. Mark then admitted that he and some other kids had damaged the back of the seats. As far as the car was concerned, we took money out of the bank account we had opened for Mark, and so did his father, and we sent the money to the father who had called. I told him since he had done some of the damage to the car, then he had to pay us back. It was a shame that no one else paid anything, but it was the right thing for us to do, and Mark knew he wasn't getting around it. My husband and I made it clear to Mark that he needed to continue seeing his counselor, and we hoped things would get better in time.

●●●

Chapter Nine

Because I was worried about Mark having too much time on his hands again, I began taking him to look for a new job. It was toward the end of his sophomore year of high school, and after putting a few applications in at different places, he managed to get a job at a local sub shop. They started off scheduling him for a couple days a week. By this time, he was ignoring us at home again and staying out until all hours. When we took things away to punish him, it felt like it did no good, as it would just make him angrier. This reaction was because of the drug addiction that he had, which we later realized.

In between all of this, we also had some good times with Mark, where everything was going well, and then it would revert back to the craziness again. It was such a roller coaster ride. After learning more about the disease of addiction, Mark's behavior all started to make sense.

I started calling Mark's father all the time, telling him about how Mark was acting at home and that he was getting detention at school on occasion. On a day while Mark was at work, Mark's father called and told me not to call Mark and that he would go up to his work to confront him face to face. When he arrived there, he said that Mark's friends were already waiting for Mark. The friends were trying to be nice to Mark's father, who wanted no part of any of them. When Mark finally left work, his father grabbed him and put him up against the car and told him that he was tired of all the phone calls he was getting from me about him, and he better straighten up and work on himself. Soon afterward, Mark lost his job because he didn't show up to work one day.

I missed my son so much; this was not the person he had always been. It made me really sad to think that it had gotten this far and we weren't able to stop it. He just kept self-destructing, and we were along for the ride. What do you do next, after you've already made several efforts to try to help your child? It really felt awful going through all of that. While all of this was going on, I still had to go to work and do my job and put a smile on my face every day and try to block out the problems, or else I wasn't able to function right.

We got through the summer, and it was time for Mark to start his junior year of high school. We were hoping for the best and keeping our fingers crossed for a good year. It was a hell of a sophomore year, and my husband and I wanted Mark to start off with a clean slate. My husband's birthday was in November, and we decided to go to where my sister lived so we could go out to dinner while my daughter was with my sister and niece. When we got back to my sister's, we were waiting for her to get home with the kids when I get a call on my cell. It was the sergeant from our local police station. He said he had my husband's car, and I told him that was impossible. He said that Mark had stolen the spare key off my key ring and had taken my husband's car out for a joyride. When Mark was driving on our street, the sergeant said Mark made a right turn, and then decided he didn't want to turn right, so he backed out onto the main road instead. This caused the sergeant, who was behind him, to swerve into the other lane, almost causing an accident. They left the car across the street from where this occurred and took Mark in to the police station.

The officer wanted me to pick Mark up at the police station, and I told him he would have to call Mark's father because we were an hour away. The officer said I should call his father, which I did. I told Mark's father that he better not bring him to our house tonight because my husband and I were furious. Lucky for Mark, there was no damage to the car. A court date was set for eight weeks later at municipal court. Mark was being charged with reckless driving, using a cell phone while driving, and driving without a license. He didn't even have a permit yet because we were holding off on that privilege because of his behavior.

I called Mark's father the day after he was brought to the police station. We talked about how we should all handle what had just happened. Now I was really getting twisted from all of this, as any parent would be. We tried to discipline him in the best way that we knew how, by grounding him, shutting down his phone, and doing whatever it took.

Chapter Ten

I was still checking Mark's room when he wasn't around. One day I went into his room and stood there, just staring at his nightstand. I looked under some papers in the back of the drawer in the nightstand and found a couple hundred dollars and a dime bag of something that turned out to be cocaine. I held onto the money and the cocaine. I was so upset that I couldn't even think straight. When I finally calmed down, I made the decision to not say anything to Mark and see what would happen when he came home. When Mark arrived home, we said a few words to each other, and he went to bed. The next morning I got up early because I couldn't sleep, and I heard Mark get up and open his drawer. I could tell he was furious as I heard him slam the drawer shut. He didn't say a word to me, but why would he, because doing so would confirm I knew what he was up to. I told my husband I thought Mark was dealing drugs again. My husband said he didn't think he would go down that path again. So I grabbed the money and cocaine and showed my husband. He opened up the dime bag. He said it was definitely cocaine and asked if I found anything else, and I told him I didn't. We threw out the cocaine, and I hid the money. I wondered if Mark knew I was the one who took the stuff from his drawer. I told Mark's father also, and he said if he is dealing drugs again, then let him get busted. That was not what I wanted to hear.

I figured that if Mark was dealing drugs again, I would find another scale in his room. Mark had asked if I had gone in his room; I told him I hadn't, and I never let on to what I was up to. I finally made the decision to call an outpatient rehab center, because now we were dealing with Mark using cocaine, after my husband and I confronted him about it, and he needed help. I set up an appointment. In the meantime I was still checking his room regularly, and sure enough, I was tearing apart his room one day—nothing until I looked under his bed and noticed the mesh part of his box spring was ripped. And when I opened it to check, I just couldn't catch my breath for a moment. I found another scale and a bag of empty dime bags. All I kept saying was, "Why, God, why? Why *my* son?" "He is such a beautiful kid, what is he doing to his life?"

This was the second scale I had found, and it was suggested by Mark's father that I call a family member on his side of the family who was in law enforcement. I called his relative that day, letting him know what was up. He said he would call Mark and tell him he wanted to take him out to dinner and talk to him.

Mark's relative arrived that evening, and the two of them went out. They discussed what I had found. A couple of hours later they came back, and he came in to talk to us while he had Mark wait in the car. He said they talked about everything that had happened, and he hoped he had made an impression on Mark to stop his harmful behavior. He told him that if the cops caught him dealing drugs, he would be arrested and he would then be in the system. He told Mark the system was awful, and he didn't want him to have to go down this path. It would be up to Mark, and we all hoped for the best. He said to allow Mark to consider it overnight and to not badger him for the rest of the night. He also said that Mark would apologize to us and that Mark needed to focus on getting help and staying away from people who were doing drugs.

When he came inside, Mark said nothing, and the fact that he didn't apologize let me know right away that what his relative was trying to tell him didn't sink in at all.

Mark knew it was wrong, but he kept experimenting with drugs on a daily basis. He was hanging out with people who did drugs and dealt them. I honestly don't know how a beautiful child like him didn't walk away from all of it. I don't know what was going on with him; it seemed like he had no fear. We weren't aware of what kind of other drugs he was experimenting with. I wasn't in denial at all, but handling it was the hard part. It really saddened me that we couldn't stop the craziness. You can't imagine what it is like until you go through it and see how a beautiful person has had a great life and a bright future ahead of him but was wasting it away. I felt I had done everything possible to help him see the light and make things better. When Mark and I were alone one day, I asked him like I had before if I had ever told him I loved him so much, and he said again that I told him every day. The addiction had taken over, and I knew that deep down Mark did not want it that way.

It was time for our appointment with the local outpatient rehab, and when we arrived, Mark and I had a talk with the director. While Mark was in another room, I was asked to speak with one of the counselors to tell her what had happened since this all began. She said he definitely qualified for treatment due to the cocaine use. My husband and I thought it would be the best thing for him, and we agreed that we would try it out, and he would have to go after school. The rehab center had a van service to pick Mark up at the high school. He went once, and the next time he had to go he tried to avoid the van, and the high school said some students saw Mark hide when the van came to pick him up. The rehab center found out and said if he wasn't going to cooperate, they were cancelling the sessions.

The next day when Mark went to school, he knew he was to be picked up at school by the drivers for the rehab center, or the "two big apes" as he called them. We thought everything was set, but that was not the case. I had the day off from work, and I called the rehab center and spoke to the counselor. I told him that I had searched Mark's room again and found dime bags of cocaine and money. I thought Mark was still dealing drugs, and I needed their help with the situation.

The counselor said he had an idea to approach Mark by making up a story that he had heard he was dealing drugs in the rehab center. He said he would take care of it for me. I told him I would call him back if Mark didn't get on the van to the rehab. I must have cried the whole morning, and when it came time for school to be over, I called the school to see if he had gotten on the van, and they told me they couldn't locate him and he had probably already left school. I called the counselor back, and he told me to make the call to the police, because he had been to too many funerals. Making that call meant I would have to have my son arrested.

I began thinking about all of our efforts to reach Mark: talking with him, writing letters to him, getting family involved to help, and seeing that nothing was working. I had to make a decision. Would I let this continue and look the other way, or was I going to try to save my son's life by having him arrested? This is not what I wanted to do; it is what I had to do. After steadily crying about it, I got the courage to make the call. That decision would forever change all of our lives.

I called the police and told them that my son was dealing drugs and he needed to be arrested. I had given him two chances, he was not listening, and we could not continue to have all this craziness going on in our lives. An officer immediately showed up, and we discussed what had been happening. The officer called a cop that was familiar with Mark's situation, and the officer that was at my house asked the cop what should be done. He was told to bust Mark. I told the officer what the counselor at the rehab center said and that he had given me the advice to have Mark arrested. I was feeling so many emotions—anger, sadness, frustration, and worry about what was going to happen now that the police would be involved. We knew nothing about how the system worked and didn't realize what we were about to encounter, but this was a matter of saving my son's life, and nothing was more important than that.

Mark showed up later, acting like nothing happened. He went up to his room, and I called the police; they arrived within minutes and went up to Mark's room and arrested him. When they brought Mark down, he looked like he was on something and didn't say much, and they took him to the police station. One of the officers told me I needed to come over to the police station in a little bit. I got there and met up with a detective. We spoke about what happened, and he asked me a few questions.

While dealing with the situation at the police station, the sergeant who was involved in the situation with Mark's reckless driving charge was at the police station and wanted to talk with me. We talked about that night when Mark had taken my husband's car out, and I told him that I didn't know whether I should laugh or cry. I told him that I thought this was so crazy and so not like Mark, and that we had a great family and couldn't understand any of this. His court date was coming up the following week at municipal court, and we would have to deal with what was going to be done about that also. The officers said I did the right thing and that they would talk to Mark, and then he would be coming home with me that night. I suggested after talking with his father that maybe he should be put in the youth detention center, but the system doesn't work like that, so it wasn't going to happen.

Mark came out to where I was waiting, and we didn't speak at all on the short ride home. I had already called my husband and told him what had happened. We just didn't know what to do. I don't think any parent is prepared for anything like this.

I remember the next day talking to Mark about all the things that had happened, telling him I knew that he didn't really want to be like that because he had always been an upstanding guy. He began crying and telling me he was sorry that he didn't turn out to be the son I had always wanted. I cried with him and told him that I loved him very much, and no matter what, that would never, ever change. I told him that his Uncle John, my brother, wanted me to ask him if he had ever heard of the saying, "wickedness was never happiness," because he said a person cannot be wicked and be happy at the same time. He did not know what to say, so I told him I wanted him to think about it.

Mark told me he had talked to some of his friends' parents, and they had said they would never have their own kid arrested. He really couldn't believe that I had him arrested. I told him that I am not like those other parents, and I really didn't care what their views were. I had given him chances already, and he had blown it. I told him that I was trying to save his life, but he didn't understand that.

A couple of weeks later, it was time for court, and Mark and I met his father at the municipal building. Mark lost his privilege to drive for six months, so he could not get a permit until then, and also he had to pay a fee. He set up a monthly payment plan, and we left court.

···

Chapter Eleven

One night my husband and I had plans to go out with people from my work, and Mark had made plans with his father. His friend that he would be going out with that night would be dropping him off at his father's house later where he would spend the night. Before we headed out, I sat down with Mark, told him to give up his house key, and told him that my husband and I were leaving and he would be leaving first. That was the plan, and there was no changing it. He seemed angry, so because of that and the way things had been going, I got curious and decided to check the downstairs windows, and some were unlocked. I knew my husband didn't do it and I didn't do it, so I relocked them. I was going to make sure there wouldn't be any parties at my house.

When it was time to leave, Mark walked out first, and we followed and got into our car. I had told him what the rules were going to be, and that was that. I saw that he was upset as he called his friend to come and get him. I called to check in with him while we were out, and he seemed to be okay. After our dinner, everyone was going back to the one couple's house for a little while, and so we went also. Around 11:00 p.m. I got a call from Mark asking when we would be home. He said the plans had changed, and he would be coming back home instead of going to his father's. It was becoming normal for Mark's plans with his father to change with little notice. We decided to cut the night short and head home. We walked in, and I noticed the light was on in our playroom and immediately saw a blanket over the back window. I pulled it off and saw that the window was completely broken. I looked down and saw tons of glass all over. I screamed for my husband, and then I took a flashlight and decided to check outside. I saw that our wrought iron table out back was dismantled, so that was probably what had been used to smash the window from the outside. I was worried where Mark was and called him, but he did not answer. When he finally came home, we were glad that he was okay but furious and wondering what all the mess was all about. After he admitted that he had broken the window and said he was sorry, I told him he would be paying for it to be replaced; his stepdad and I weren't paying a penny of it.

Mark had a school event to go to a couple of weeks later, and when he got back, he was acting overly nice to me, and I became suspicious. Obviously, we were having issues with trusting him, and he knew I was always suspicious of him, which I know bothered him.

I had seen Mark take off his jacket in the playroom, and I decided to check it out. I walked into the room, and hoped I was wrong and that I wouldn't find anything. I waited until Mark was in his bedroom. I first checked the outside pockets and found nothing. Then I remembered it had an inside pocket. As I opened the jacket I saw there was something in the inside pocket, and my heart just sank. It turned out to be a bag of marijuana and some money. I was so upset but went up to my room and hid it. Later on I heard Mark on the phone, and he went into the playroom and shut the door. I was shaking by now and did not want to say anything to my husband because I knew he would immediately blow up at Mark, and it wouldn't do any good anyway.

In the meantime I heard Mark searching the whole room and acting really mad. He came up to my room and asked me what I did with his stuff.

So I asked him, "What stuff? What stuff are you talking about?" And I said that I had no idea what he meant. He didn't know how to answer me, so he kept saying that he knew I had his stuff, and then he said that my husband probably had it. So then my husband came up because he heard Mark badgering me, and he told Mark to stop bothering me. Finally Mark gave up asking and went back on the phone with someone. I really wanted to tell my husband about it at that moment, but I didn't.

The next morning Mark missed the bus, and I asked him what was going on. He said he didn't want to go to school because someone at school lent him money, and he couldn't pay the person back like he had promised. Mark then asked if I could take money out of his bank account to repay the kid. I asked him why he owed some kid money, just to see what he would say. He said it was money he had to repay the kid for when they had been out and the other kid had paid. I told him I would get the money back, but I knew I wasn't actually going to. I told him I was leaving to go to the bank but decided instead to take my daughter to lunch and make a call to the police station while out to let them know I was coming in to the police station. At this point I was fed up, and Mark wasn't listening, so I needed to take action. I brought the marijuana and money to the police station and told them what had happened. Mark was still at home waiting. I told the cops what happened, and the officer asked me if I wanted to press charges. I really didn't want to, but it was the right thing to do since I didn't have another solution. One of the cops picked him up and brought him in. They told him they remembered him, as he was just in there a few weeks earlier. I kept thinking what a mess this all was. Mark just couldn't stop the addiction he had.

There would be a hearing the next day in front of the judge. I spoke to his father, and he could not make the hearing, so Mark and I went by ourselves. The judge ordered a drug test. It came out positive for marijuana, cocaine, and PCP. I was shocked when he mentioned PCP. We went back in front of the judge about a half hour later, and the judge told him he was disturbed with the results of the test.

Mark told the judge he had never done PCP, and the judge told him that the marijuana that he bought off the street was probably laced with PCP because that is what the drug sellers typically do. At the end of the hearing, the judge put Mark on house arrest. This would mean he would be wearing an ankle monitor and he could go to school but would have to go home afterward. If he had a job, he would have to give the times that he was working, but he could not go out and socialize. This was really annoying because the parent had to call the times in, and we had to have a schedule, but if it meant Mark would straighten out, I was willing to do what it took to help my son. Weeks had gone by, and when he was finally off the ankle monitor, he was set up with a behavioral care service, ordered by the judge. This was a free service that links clients to community mental health resources. The Judge wanted a court-ordered psychiatric evaluation for Mark in December 2006. This center was supposed to help set up court-ordered outpatient drug treatment.

It was decided that we would try the outpatient rehab again, and this time Mark cooperated with the plan. He had individual meetings as well as group meetings. He said all the kids in the group meetings were really fascinated with his stories of how he dealt drugs. My husband and Mark's father and Mark and I had met with the director of the place. She told Mark she wished he would use his entrepreneurial skills for a bright future for himself rather than drugs. She also said he was such a smart kid and should stay focused on being around good people who want to do well in life.

I thought this would finally be the end of all the craziness. He was testing clean from drugs, so we adults thought that maybe, just maybe, we were seeing some improvement toward him really getting better.

Chapter Twelve

Because he completed the program at the outpatient rehab center, we gave Mark a chance to redeem himself. Not too long after this, he started staying out late again and not picking up his phone at times and punishment wasn't really working. People in the family were giving their input about it, but I asked them what they would like us to do. He wasn't getting along with my husband, due to what was going on again, and the fights started again between my husband and me about that. Mark's dad was getting disgusted and said "Let him get busted, or kick him out of the house if he keeps messing up." Even though I was mad too, I wasn't about to look the other way. You still have to keep on trying to guide young people in the right direction.

I called the behavioral center for advice, and they told me he could be put in a shelter so that he would be away from the kids he was hanging out with and would be safe. They also recommended a children's youth service that I could call who could help with his behavior.

In the meantime, because Mark was missing days at school again, I had the vice principal order drug tests, and I took Mark to the lab. It came out positive for drugs, and the vice principal sent a letter home saying Mark was now expelled from school, and a meeting was set up to determine what would be done now. Mark's father and I sat with Mark at this meeting with the principal, vice principal, and counselor at the high school to discuss the situation. I let them know things had been so crazy, this was not our Mark, and he had always been a great kid. He had always done well in school, but I had noticed his grades were slipping a little and that drugs were affecting him to the point that we didn't know what to do anymore.

It became court ordered that Mark would be put in an inpatient rehab clinic about forty-five minutes away for a while. He had to agree that he needed help, and all the necessary paperwork would be done by the children's youth service. He knew he needed help, but I know he didn't want to leave and go live there for a while. It was a shame because the month he had to leave we had received a letter stating that in honor of Mark's academic achievement and leadership ability, he was invited to participate in the National Young Leaders Conference to represent the state of New Jersey as a National Scholar at the 2007 National Leaders Conference to be held that summer in Washington, D.C. This was such a great honor, and we were so proud of him, but Mark could not go because he needed help, and that was the most important thing. Some of these missed opportunities were really devastating to me.

Just before this session of rehab, there was another missed opportunity that was brought up, as there was a baseball team forming that wasn't part of the high school, but they would be playing on the field at Mark's high school, and some of his old teammates were in the league. While driving with Mark one night passing by the baseball field, he looked over at the field and told me that he really missed it. I thought it would be a great idea for him to join the league and made the payment, only to find out he was going to be getting inpatient care and he would have to leave as soon as the papers were signed. It would have been great for him to be part of a team again, but he had an addiction that playing baseball would not take away, and treating it was the top priority now.

At the time all of this craziness was going on, we really didn't know a lot about addiction or what happened in the rehab programs and outpatient care, but we were willing to try anything. We didn't know at the time how hard it was for a person to stop using drugs. Now we know a lot about what an addiction is all about, how the brain really changes when a person has an addictive personality. From the experience of dealing with Mark, I know now that when a person becomes addicted, they can be angry a lot of the time and take it out on the people who love them. It is not an easy thing to kick that habit. Mark probably thought we were trying to ruin his life at first; he didn't really understand that we were trying to save it. I didn't want this new rehab program to be a punishment thing. I wanted it to be a helpful and healing process, one that he would embrace, and hopefully it would help him understand that if he continued on the path that he was going on, things would only get worse.

In March the family service specialist gave me a list of what he would need for his stay, and we bagged it all up. She picked us up a few days later, and we headed to the rehab center. It was paid for by the courts, and being a little reluctant about state run places, I was hopeful it would be a good recovery place. When we arrived, his father had come also with his wife and their son, and we all met with our family service specialist. We were told that he would continue his education there, and there were teachers there to help him do that. We had to say our good-byes, and it really felt terrible. I was sad that it had come this far. Not knowing how it would be for him there and what kind of kids he was going to be around made me uneasy. We were told there was a period where there would be no contact with Mark at first, and then he would be able to call us. All I kept thinking about was, "What was my son thinking, was he going to be okay, and were they going to treat him well?"

When we finally heard from Mark, it was so good to hear from him, but he didn't sound good at all. He told us that one of the kids there had stolen some of his clothes in the laundry room. He didn't really like the kids and kept to himself. I just kept thinking, "Why is this happening to him?" I was really worried about him, wondering how he was going to get better being around these kinds of kids. Mark said the other patients thought everything was a joke, and he felt that it wasn't helping him get better at all. A couple of them were trying to act like they were serious in the group sessions, and then when the counselor left, they would laugh, saying that they didn't care about getting well. I tried to tell him not to worry about the other kids; he should just worry about himself. It wasn't about them anyway. I told him the sooner he worked on himself, the sooner he would be done with rehab, and they would let him out as long as they felt he was doing well and completed the program.

We had conferences set up, the first one being after thirty days of entry, with the counselor. There was one scheduled each month. At first Mark was not embracing the whole thing, but as time went on, he started doing really well. I think he still thought marijuana was just a plant that you smoke, and it wasn't considered a drug and it was not addicting. They were trying to show him that he had to work on himself, and I'm sure he met other kids who had tried things worse than cocaine and marijuana. Schoolwise he did great, as usual, and he was even allowed to come to his sister's communion luncheon, which we were really happy about. While I was driving Mark back to rehab the day of the communion, he started getting upset, saying he just wanted to be home with us. He did not like it there. I told him we all missed him a lot, but we had been through so much, and all we wanted was for him to work on himself and get well. By the time the counselors were ready to okay him to leave rehab, it was the end of July, so he had stayed there four and a half months.

When the case worker and I picked him up, he was still really upset that he had been put there. He said there were no therapeutic things there like the brochure had described, and he mostly sat around and did a whole lot of nothing. When I heard this, I was unhappy but thought that maybe he would realize what he had done and would not want to get into trouble again. Little did I know that he had a more serious addiction than we thought. If it had been an easy thing for him to stop his addiction, I know Mark would have stopped.

Mark was also talking about maybe living with his father but later changed his mind and told me he said this out of anger. He really just wanted to be normal again and do the right thing.

I called the principal at the high school and told him that Mark was out of rehab now, and if we couldn't get him into another school we were looking into, he would have to come back to this high school for senior year. The counselor at the high school did not think it was the best thing for him, as the negative influences were still there and Mark might be influenced again. When we found out that a private school couldn't take him, I got a note from the inpatient rehab center that he was ready to start high school again. So a month later, when summer was over, there was no choice but to go back and start his senior year of high school.

···

Chapter Thirteen

We had already started family counseling once a week through the children's youth service, and the counselor would come to our house. Senior year had begun, and we thought Mark was off to a good start. But one day when he was in the shower before school, I had come upstairs to get something from the closet next to the bathroom and heard the shower running, but I heard Mark talking to someone on his cell phone. I heard things that sounded like he was reverting back to his old ways, and as soon as he was done getting ready, I confronted him. I told him, "Get out of my house and get to school!", and he asked why I was so angry at him. I told him that I had heard him on the phone unintentionally, and he asked what I heard, and I told him I heard enough to know that I thought something was going on again, and I could no longer trust him anymore. I was upset that he had been out of rehab such a short time, and I didn't feel I could trust him. He then said, "My life sucks!" "My whole life is about probation and counseling, and I can't stand it anymore and I just want to be normal again!"

I said "I love you, but you have made some bad choices, and you will have to decide whether you are going to do well or mess up again." "It will be your decision; it is your life!" I think it helped that I called him out on this. I said, "It would be a waste of our time to have all of this counseling if you are going back to your old ways." He said, "I will work on myself, and I am going to make you proud!"

After that conversation, things seemed to be much better. After a month of school, Mark called me up one day while I was at work. He said I was going to be so proud of him because he got called down to the office, and they told him he was the student of the month. The tears of happiness started flowing, and I said, "Congratulations, I am so proud of you!" "Keep it up, because you are going to get in to the college that you want if you maintain excellent grades." He wanted to go to a certain school that was one of the top ten universities on the East Coast, and I knew he had a chance with an amazing first-quarter report card and good SAT scores, in addition to having good grades the other years. He applied during the early application period and sent in his SAT scores and the grades he had so far.

He also applied to another college that we toured, but it was farther away. He wasn't sure if he was going to be as happy there, but we wanted to see what they were offering because his grades were good enough for a huge academic scholarship. He wanted to go for the business program and possibly be a financial planner, but he said he might change to another business career if he felt it wasn't for him. We were just happy that he was headed in the right direction now. He had been through so much with outpatient counseling, probation, trying to get through school, dealing with the same people around him, and the family counseling we were getting. He was following his curfew, helping out at the house, and doing things for us without being asked. There were definitely some improvements coming out of rehab, but the trust issue was not changing. I was afraid every time he went out that there was a possibility he could go back to his old ways and the same friends who were not good influences. I knew we couldn't make him stay home on the weekends. We stressed the importance of hanging out with the right people and getting involved in after-school activities. He brought up joining student council, and I thought it was a good idea, so he decided to join. He said he wished he had gotten involved in after-school activities instead of hanging around with people that weren't good for him the other years of high school, but I told him not to look back and to move forward. I told him what's done is done, and it was important to continue to work on staying straight, even with the negative influences around him. By January of senior year, we only saw an occasional friend over, but Mark had a girlfriend since January of his senior year and spent a lot of time with her. Mark mentioned that nobody really wanted to come over because they thought they might get arrested. So I told Mark maybe some of his friends weren't any good then and told him I was glad that they weren't coming over.

Now it was February, and we were waiting for college acceptance letters in the mail. I got the call one day when I was at work. Mark called me and said, "Mom, guess what, I got into the university that I wanted, and I also got an academic scholarship!" I was screaming and flipping out at work. I congratulated him and told him how proud I was and that I knew he could do it. I wish I was there with him when he opened the letter to share that moment with him. It was a really good day, one of the happiest days in a long time. He then called my husband and his father to share the good news, and they were really excited too. When he had called my parents, they cried and were really happy, too. My son was going to college, and he had come a long way. To surprise him, I went out and bought a dozen balloons with the message "congrats" written on them. I surprised him, and we just hugged each other, and I cried my eyes out. This was really a special moment for both of us. The whole family was so excited for him.

Then the next letter came in. He was accepted to the other college with a huge academic scholarship, but he chose to go to the school he wanted to go to more. His mind was made up. He knew what he wanted, and he promised he would get involved at the college, especially in baseball, which he had always loved.

...

Chapter Fourteen

A short time after the college acceptance news, my husband went to his car for something early one morning, and he noticed a big dent in his car and a blown-out tire. My husband was so upset, thinking someone had vandalized the car. I took a look and thought the same thing at first. I decided to wake Mark up and ask him if he knew what happened, and he said he had no idea. He went out with me to look, and we came back in the house without saying much.

My husband decided that we would call the police to make a report. The officer arrived and took a look at the car. He said he knew the car had been driven; he had seen this type of thing many times in his career. We didn't know who took it out for sure, or maybe because Mark had been doing so well, we were in denial about it. The officer said that the car may have been in an accident, and until we found out who did it, he would have to write up a report.

At this point in our regular family counseling sessions, we were told that we needed to start trusting Mark because it was driving him crazy that we didn't. Every time he left the house since he came out of rehab, I would ask him who he would be going out with, and I would always remind him to stay on the straight path. His past behavior drove me to ask all the time.

I brought Mark in to the police station because the officer wanted to talk to him about the car. Mark said he didn't know anything about the damage to the car, and he was sticking to his story. The officer had me read something about falsifying information and that a ticket would be issued to my husband since it was his car. We still didn't know what was going on yet. Mark and I drove home, and when I told my husband what the officer said, he said no way was he going to get a ticket, and my husband said he and I were taking a drive back to the station to discuss this with the police.

When we got there, we met with the officer and the chief of police. They believed that Mark took it out without a doubt, and we said maybe he let his girlfriend drive the car and he didn't want to tell us. I told them we would give them a call after discussing it with Mark. We sat down with Mark, and then told him what was said and that he better start talking. He told us that two kids had come over while we were sleeping and that when he fell asleep on the couch, they stole my husband's keys and took the car out for a joyride. I just looked at him and asked if he expected us to believe this story. I told him that if that was the story, he could tell the officer himself. So I called the officer back and told him Mark wanted to tell him what happened, and the officer showed up at our house soon afterward.

So the four of us sat at the kitchen table, and Mark told the officer what he had told us. The officer said he didn't believe a word of it, and when Mark mentioned a couple of names to the officer, he told Mark he thought he recognized one of them. He also mentioned that if he found out he was wasting his time trying to chase around kids that didn't even exist, he would press charges against Mark. I told him we had spent a good part of the day trying to get the real story. Before the officer left, he said he would have to write up the report within a few days. Mark looked sad and started crying, and we were just saddened by the whole thing. I wasn't going to yell at him. I wanted the real truth to come out, so I thought, "This time I'm not going to say anything more and I'll just see what Mark does."

We were following what the family counselor had said about the trust issue, and the next day it was time for school. I told Mark I would drive him to school that morning, and he was unusually quiet the whole way there. It was going to be up to Mark to tell the truth. I thought he knew right from wrong. A few minutes after I got home, I got a call from Mark, who was crying and saying he needed to be picked up. He wanted to go to the police station to tell the real story. I knew he had a conscience that was getting to him, and the truth was finally going to come out now.

I immediately picked him up and told Mark he was a real dummy because this would have been avoided if he would have told the truth in the first place. He said he was scared to tell us because we were all in counseling and things had been going so well. He told me that he knew it was wrong to take my husband's keys and take the car out, yet he did it anyway but didn't know why.

Mark told the police officer and me that he had met up with some friends on a rainy night. There was a traffic circle in one of the neighborhoods, and as he was driving around it, he skidded and went right up on the curb. He was actually able to drive the car home without being noticed, but by the time he pulled into the driveway, the whole tire was destroyed. Again, I didn't know whether to laugh or cry at this point. We were on such an emotional rollercoaster ride. One day we would be laughing, having a good time with Mark, and the next we were angry and frustrated at him. It was just such a crazy time of our lives, and it is amazing I didn't have a nervous breakdown. The officer asked me if I coerced Mark into telling the truth, and I told her no. Nothing came of it. Mark wanted to apologize to the officer for not telling the truth the first time. I told him not to bother, as it would stir things up again. It was better to just let it go.

At our counseling session, the social worker stopped over also to see how everything was going, and Mark told her what had happened. She wasn't mad, and she told him that everyone lies—adults lie too—but he needed to work on telling the truth in the future. She was so proud of him for getting the scholarship. We were all trying to concentrate on the positive things he was now doing and not the negative.

● ● ●

Chapter Fifteen

We had not let Mark get his permit for a long time because we didn't trust him, with good reason. But everything else was going really well, so I let him apply for his license. His father had plans to get him a car if everything went well, which was a good incentive for him to do the right thing. The first time he failed the driver's test, so we had to wait a couple of weeks for him to take it again. It was another setback for Mark and very frustrating for him, as he was set on driving that day. I told him two weeks wasn't going to hurt him, and so we went back again, and he passed. All I thought about was that now he didn't have to be picked up by any friend, which I hated anyway.

He was given his car, and even though it wasn't brand new, it was his own. He went to a local convenience store he had worked at before he had gone to the inpatient rehab center. He was totally honest with them about what had happened with him, and because they liked him so much, he asked for them to give him another chance, and he got his job back. His father said if there was any trouble, the car would be sold, and there would not be another car for Mark. He did end up losing the job not too long afterward. I never got the true story as to why they let him go.

As the weeks went by, we were focusing on another great day: a scholarship banquet for the university Mark would be going to. My husband and I went, along with Mark and his girlfriend. It was a good night, and we hadn't been so happy in a long time. I was trying to stay focused on this great opportunity that Mark had, but I was also still being cautious because the trust issue was still there, and I was still questioning things at home at times. Despite what I was feeling, the whole family was rooting for Mark, and we couldn't wait until orientation day at the university.

The night after the scholarship banquet, I had just gotten back from the gym when I pulled into my driveway and was approached by several police officers. They had a warrant to search the house. They had been watching Mark and others for a couple of months, and they said he was selling drugs again, and they were looking for him. I told them Mark said he was meeting someone and would be back later. I had left Mark a message on his cell before I got out of my car, telling him it was getting really late and he needed to be home now.

The police then came into our house; my daughter was already asleep, and I woke up my husband. They told him why they were there, and he looked stunned. I was so disappointed. I told my husband that I had a feeling something was up, but every time I would tell him Mark was up to something, he would always say that he didn't think so and that I was exaggerating, and then I would find something. I told my husband that in the future he needed to stop saying that nothing was going on because it always backfired on us.

The police officers tore up Mark's room and searched other places in our house too, but they did not find any drugs. They asked me if I had any idea of where he might be, and I told them I didn't. I tried calling Mark after they had finished their search, and he actually picked up. I asked him where he was, and he said he was at a local diner applying for a job, which he really was. He said he would be home soon. After our conversation, the police left to confront Mark. After finding him at the diner, they walked him out of the building and began searching his car. They found drug paraphernalia and a digital scale. This was a violation of his probation, so they confiscated his car, and he was released to us and was brought home. Two other kids had been arrested after the police raided their homes.

When Mark got home, I couldn't even speak to him; the hurt was so great, and I did not know what I was going to do next. I had to let it all sink in first. When we did talk, I needed to ask him what was going on. Did he realize that graduation from high school was coming up and then college? He didn't know how to respond. He knew he was caught and there were no excuses to be made.

Every time you pick up a charge, you have to appear before the judge. All I was thinking at that moment was, "Oh no, we have to go back to court again. I can't take this anymore." We had been there so many times already, and it was getting very annoying. Sometimes when we went, we waited outside the courtroom until his name was called, only to find out the court date was cancelled and had to be rescheduled for some reason. We sometimes had to wait for hours there. Luckily I had the most wonderful, understanding boss who allowed me to take time off for every court date. It was just me, Mark, and our lawyer every time we went to court.

We had no clue that Mark had been taking pills—ecstasy, Xanax, and others. We later found out he had tried magic mushrooms, too. At this point Mark was still continuing his probation, and he was being drug tested regularly also. If the test had come up positive, we would have known about it. I learned later on how a person can get around drug tests. Also, he was going weekly to another outpatient facility recommended by the court. We were so beside ourselves with grief, anger, and frustration. We were trying to learn to trust him through our family counseling, but I knew his addiction was too great. Someone once asked me, "What about a person's free will?" I told him that I believe you lose control of your free will when you are heavily addicted.

Once the outpatient care program was completed, the counselor felt confident that Mark was on the right track and everything would be better for him. You get to a point where you just want everything to be fine, and you want to forget that all of the insanity has been a reality. Now my husband and I had to discuss whether or not we were still going to send him to college. The loans were already in place, and I kept thinking that if he got away from the crowd he had been associating with and met new people at the university, it would be a lot better for him. Since his car was gone at this point and Mark knew he would have to rely on getting rides again, which he hated, I thought he would wise up. He had this amazing opportunity with college, and we were all rooting for him and not about to give up on him. If we made the decision to not allow him to go away to college, then he would still be around the same crowd, which we did not want.

My sister, my husband, and I went to the awards night at the high school, and Mark was awarded a special achievement award through student council for outstanding leadership to the school. I was so happy, but I had mixed emotions because I couldn't understand how a child could do so well and then go and do illegal stuff.

My husband, Pasquale, Mark, and I, high school awards ceremony, 2008

● ● ●

Chapter Sixteen

Mark's graduation was a really great day. We loved Mark so much and were concentrating on all the good things happening. He graduated with another President's Award for Academic Excellence, the same type of award he had received at his eighth grade graduation, in addition to his academic scholarship. We were so excited for him, as he really did try to turn his life around despite what had happened recently. We told Mark to stay on the straight path and that he had so much going for him right now with college coming up, and we encouraged him not to ruin the good thing he had going.

We had a party for him, and everyone was so excited about college and the scholarship, so I didn't tell my family about the raiding of the house incident. We were told by the family counselor just to keep it between Mark's father and us because everyone would have an opinion about it, and it would create more drama we did not need. When he was asked by the family where his car was, Mark said his dad was keeping it at his house for now, and anyway, the college would not allow a car on campus for your first and second year.

A couple of months later, Mark called me and said he went into the police station and asked them if he could have his car back. They were probably astounded that he would have the guts to go in there and ask for his car back, and I couldn't believe it myself when he told me. The police called Mark's lawyer at this time. He left without his car and had to wait to see what they were going to do. Weeks later after going into the police station, Mark was finally told he was going to get his car back. His father went over to the police station, and they said they would be keeping their eye on Mark still. We were convinced that he was going to start fresh, go to college, meet new friends, and put this all behind him. It's amazing how convincing a person can be when they are hooked on drugs. There were so many apologies from Mark, and who wouldn't want to believe their own kid? But he kept going. It was his strong addiction, and there was no turning back.

Orientation day at the college was a great day. We got to see more of the campus and meet lots of other parents whose children would be freshmen. It was such a beautiful campus, and I was looking forward to being on the mother's guild there, which I thought was a great idea to be connected to the college.

Mark, Madeira Beach, Florida, summer of 2008, our last family vacation with him

As the summer days went by, we were picking up things here and there Mark would need for his dorm room at college, and it was about a month before college started on a late afternoon. Mark said he was going out and would be right back, his famous line. By that time we were trying to trust him and didn't say a word when he left. I was trying to establish some type of normalcy in our lives. He was to pick up his girlfriend not too long after he left but apparently never showed up to get her.

I received a call that I needed to come down to a police station by 6:00 p.m. but not to our local station. I was in shock again, and I went immediately to go pick him up. The officer on duty spoke with me before they brought him out and said he was pulled over for weaving on the road. When they pulled him over, the officer said his car reeked of marijuana. They searched his car and found heroin and marijuana. When they mentioned heroin, I didn't know what to say.

The officer who came out to speak with me said Mark's car was still pulled off to the side of the road on a nearby highway. The officer didn't feel that it added up, a smart kid getting scholarships to colleges and doing all of this.

Mark was released to me, and we walked out. Now the probation department would find out, which would be a violation again, and there would be another court date again. I just didn't know what to say or how to react anymore. Mark didn't know what to say to me either. He obviously had an addiction to dealing drugs, on top of being addicted to using them, but he kept being tested and coming out clean. I didn't know what the signs were of heroin use, and I would have found out if he failed a drug test, so I thought that he was just selling, but that did not make it any better. Mark's father and a relative in law enforcement decided to go pick up the car, and Mark's father sold the car because of what Mark had done. Mark had already been warned, and he had blown the chance he had been given.

My husband and I didn't know what to think, and we weren't about to get anyone else in our family involved besides Mark's father and his wife because we knew what would happen if we did. Everyone would give their opinion about the situation, and we had enough heartache already; it was really starting to get unbearable. Mark had already spent time in a rehab, and we wondered what he had actually learned in that place, given that he was arrested twice after leaving. It just seemed like every time we felt confident that Mark was starting to do well, it would backfire on us. This was a pattern of his addiction, but didn't realize that until much later. If we had known more about drug addiction, maybe we would have realized the pattern earlier.

Mark was not eighteen yet, so this was all considered a juvenile charge. When the probation officer stopped over to discuss the matter, she told him to make himself proud, and us, and not to mess up the good thing that he would have at college. We had all these hopes and dreams for him to get a good education there and eventually get a good job someday.

He moved into college on Labor Day weekend. When we got there, we didn't feel anything but happiness that Mark had finally made it to college. We had the hope that he was going to start fresh and meet new people. There were some kids from his high school that he knew were also attending that my husband and I thought were decent kids. Some of the kids that we knew had been bad influences were still back home, and Mark's girlfriend was a year behind him, so we knew it would still be a challenge for him. In the summer Mark had said that he needed to get away from all of the kids he was around and that no one was any good. I told him good things were going to happen and to stay focused and start fresh.

We finally got into his room and met his roommates and their parents and set him up. I know Mark just wanted to break free and be normal, and everything had been so up and down for the past few years, but it would be up to him as to how he wanted his future to be. After taking him to lunch and talking about what we expected from him and mentioning how lucky he was to be at this college, we felt really good about how he responded to our talk.

The last stop before dropping Mark off at his room was getting the things he needed at the college bookstore. As we were headed there, I heard Mark on the phone with someone saying he would get something somewhere else. I, of course, questioned him about what I heard, and he denied it and said that he was really tired of my questioning him all the time. It was really making him nuts. We were having such a great day, so I let it go and thought maybe I was really losing it now from all we had been through. I hated always being suspicious of my child, but that's how it had been for the past three years, so it was hard not to be. We got all the things we needed to at the bookstore, and when we were done, we said our good-byes, and my husband and I left.

On the way home, my husband and I discussed that this would be a really good change for Mark, and we knew he really wanted to be at that college. The only problem was that his girlfriend lived back home, and if he was going to be coming home a lot to see her, we weren't sure how this was going to work out as a way for Mark to change his life. He also didn't have his car anymore, so he would have to get rides home to see her.

Chapter Seventeen

The university held their first mother's guild meeting, and it was great meeting a lot of new people. I met Mark afterward, we had some lunch, and he seemed to be excited that he was there. He said he had met some new kids, and he liked all the teachers in his business classes. He joined the baseball team there, and I was so excited that we were going to be able to watch him play a sport that he really loved. I thought we were finally getting back to the old Mark now.

The next time I saw Mark on campus was the family day they had, and some of my extended family came also. When we met up, there was something strange when I looked into my son's eyes, and there was a dark look about him. I knew something was up right away, but I tried not to draw attention to it. I didn't want to talk about it in front of family. I thought maybe he had been drinking the night before.

When I got home I talked to my husband about it, and he said he noticed something was up with Mark too. We talked about having an intervention. We didn't want to be accusatory, but we were concerned about Mark. Mark's father was supposed to be at family day also, but there was a miscommunication and he didn't go. I called Mark and asked him what was going on earlier, and he told me he had been drinking the night before and was just wiped out. I wasn't sure that it was really alcohol that gave him that look, so my husband and I thought that the best thing to do was to tell his father that we needed to act now to confront Mark. We were also aware that there were counselors on the campus willing to help anyone that needed it.

It was a challenge for all of us to get together to meet with Mark, as we all were on different schedules. I told Mark's father to call him and see when he had free time at night since his father had not been on the campus ever, and then we would all meet. Mark didn't return his calls, so it was put off. As the week went by, there was some good news. Mark told us he started a job on campus that he was getting paid for. We thought that was a good idea, and my husband mentioned that he wanted Mark to start paying for his own cell phone now. I told him, absolutely not because then I wouldn't be able to track him.

I was worried but trying to figure out what to do next, as we knew Mark was still being monitored by a probation officer. One time when he came home for a night and I was bringing him back to school the next day, it was just the two of us, and after arriving on campus, I stopped the car. I said, "Look around at this beautiful campus." "It could be all taken away in a flash if you are not staying on the right path, and remember what I said." I had given him so many warnings that I was sounding like a broken record at times. But this is how our lives had been for the past few years, so how could I not be like this with him? Everything that had happened affected my husband and Mark's father and me. He assured me he was doing well. He was glad he had a job on campus and was looking into another one in case the other one didn't work out. We got him new gear for baseball, which he would be starting soon, and we really couldn't wait to see the games.

I just believed that things would get better in time, and we were focusing on all the positive things going on with Mark now. It was starting to get better when we talked over the phone, and he said he really loved it there. He was still seeing his girlfriend, which was tough for both of them because he was trying to get used to college life while knowing that she was back home. I told him he needed to get involved in everything on the campus he could to keep busy and make sure he did well in his classes, because he had to keep up a certain GPA in order to keep his scholarship.

One day out of the blue, I got a call from my sister that someone called her to tell her she had Mark's phone. My sister gave me the woman's number, and I called her right away. She said she worked in the sheriff's department in our county, and while she was on the train, she saw that Mark had gotten off at a stop then realized he left his phone on the seat. The doors had already shut, so she picked up the cell phone and called the first number she saw in his phone, which was my sister's number. I asked her what stop she found it at, and I wasn't even sure where that was, as I don't really ride the speed line, and I didn't know all the stops that it made anyway. I called my husband to ask him where this stop was. I knew right away that it was a town where people were known to go and buy drugs. I was really fuming and could not wait until Mark called.

About a half hour later, I got a call from Mark saying he was on his way home. He told me he wanted to surprise me and come home for a little bit, and then he was going to see his girlfriend. I told him what had just happened with the phone and that the woman who found it would be dropping it off here in a little bit. Mark said she was wrong about what stop he got off at. According to him, it got lost one stop before the stop near our house, and then he told me that he would be home shortly. Did he think I had half a brain? I definitely believed this lady when she told me the story, and with the track record Mark had for lying, I knew his story wasn't right. I said, "There is no way possible that it was one stop before our area!" "If that was the case, how come you aren't home yet, and why would you be getting off one stop before you're supposed to? This made absolutely no sense, and he knew I was going to get to the bottom of it. I remember writing a letter to him once saying that he was never going to be able to pull one over on me because I had always wanted to work for the FBI.

Mark told me he would be home in a few minutes, which turned into more like forty-five minutes. When he got home, I had the phone, and I wanted him to come clean with the story because it didn't add up. He said he got off one stop early and got a ride home. I knew he wasn't telling the truth so I again asked him to come clean. He was in total denial, and then he said he was going to go over his girlfriend's house soon because we were fighting too much and he had to get away from me.

Mark went up to his room, and when he went into the bathroom to get ready, I checked out his room to see if I could find anything. I found a heroin needle and a dime bag of heroin, and it gave me a sick feeling, but at first I wasn't sure what kind of drug it was. I confronted him when he was ready to leave. By this time my sister was over, and she was trying to help me figure out what to do. I was trying to stay calm. I felt really heartbroken and worried for him. It was really tearing me up inside, but I still had hope. Even after reading the signs of what to look out for when a person is using this drug, we had not seen any in Mark. But someone who becomes an addict can hide his or her addiction very well. As far as we knew, if he had tested positive this past summer, the probation office would have let us know.

Mark asked where the needle and the drugs were, and I told him I had them, and he wouldn't be getting them back. He was using the old excuse, saying it wasn't his; he was holding it for a friend and needed it back.

He started freaking out, thinking I was going to call the cops again, and I told him we needed to discuss what was going on here. He wouldn't talk until I got rid of the heroin, so in front of him and my sister, down the toilet it went. He wanted to crush the needle, too, so my sister told me to just let him stomp on it, so he did. Now he was crying and screaming and said, "You are ruining my whole life!" I yelled right back at him and said, "I am not ruining your life—you are ruining your own life!" I said, "I love you so much and that later on you will understand why I keep calling you out on things that you are doing wrong."

I knew he was headed over to his girlfriend's house, and I could not let this go. Concerned that it was something we could no longer handle by ourselves, I called my father and he told me to go over to the girlfriend's house and confront Mark there.

I left right away and knocked on the girlfriend's door. I really didn't care at this point who knew. The only thing I was concerned about was my son and what could happen if I didn't address this. Her parents were at home at the time, and when Mark came in the room, I asked him in front of his girlfriend and her parents if he wanted to die because that was where he was headed if he stayed on the path he was on now. He kept denying it and denying it. And when you are that deep into using drugs, that is what you do—you try to lie as best as you can to get out of a situation. His girlfriend's stepfather saw needle marks on Mark's arms and told Mark he was not allowed to see his daughter anymore until he sought help. Again, Mark still denied he was using any drugs, even though there were visible marks. This is all part of a person's addiction.

It was time for us to leave, as the girl's mother had to be somewhere, and Mark got up and left and started walking down the street. I got in my car, and his girlfriend chased after him. He was upset and crying, but did he really think I was going to turn the other way? You don't walk away from someone you love or pretend that something bad isn't happening. I wasn't about to let that happen, and I did what I thought was the best thing at the time. I was good at confrontations now, and Mark knew I meant business. He came home, picked up some of his things, and went back to college that night. We didn't speak the rest of the weekend, and my sister called and told me he had called her crying about the situation. He told her he was mad I had confronted him in front of his girlfriend's parents because now they knew what was going on.

I was so distraught about what had happened I could not even think straight anymore. Later in the week when we spoke, he apologized and tried to assure me he would work on himself. I wished we could have done the intervention back when we had visited Mark on family day and noticed something was wrong.

We made another attempt to try to set up a meeting with Mark. He didn't return any of his father's calls, and I kept telling his father we needed to act on it now. But it was already too late. The following week I got a call from my sister that Mark had been arrested in his dorm for attempting to sell marijuana.

At first Mark was told that he would not be arrested if he gave up the drugs, which he had admitted were his. We wished it would have been handled differently, but he was taken down to the local police station wearing his pajamas. I was at lunch with people from my job when I got the call. I immediately started freaking out and told the girls to tell my boss I had to leave for the rest of the day. I got in my car and drove home to wait and see what was being done. Now that he was eighteen and not considered a juvenile anymore, he would have a record. I was so sad now, and I just couldn't believe what was happening to my beautiful son.

Later in the evening, Mark was kicked out of the police station. Mark said he was standing outside in his pajamas, trying to figure out what to do next, and everything he had was back in his dorm room. He asked an officer outside of the police station if he could take him back to his dorm for the night and so he did, as he was permitted by the school to spend the night there. I was told by the school Mark would be calling me to pick him up in the morning along with all of his things. He obviously knew that he was temporarily kicked out of college, his probation officer was going to find out what happened, and he was going to be in deep trouble now.

I don't know if he was even aware of all the conse-quences of his actions; he must have been so out of his mind, messed up on drugs. When I came the next day to pick him up with all of his belongings, he had his head down. He did not say a word, and I didn't say anything to him either at first. I was still trying to take all of it in. As we were driving away, I heard him say he couldn't believe he gave up college for heroin and cried most of the way home. I had a sick feeling inside about all of this, and I just did not know what to say to my son.

I phoned our lawyer when we arrived home, and he asked if we would stop by his office to discuss what had happened. While waiting for our lawyer, Mark appeared to be so uncomfortable; his body was aching badly, prob-ably from withdrawal, and he did not look well. I asked our lawyer if he would take on the new charge for us, and he accepted. When we finally got home, we sat outside for a little bit. I looked into Mark's eyes, and he just looked totally lost. I could not believe this had happened. I gave him a tight hug, but then I had to walk away for a little bit so I could burst out crying.

When we got home, I started to read more about heroin on the Internet. I read how an addict uses heroin in differ-ent ways. One way to use the drug is to inject yourself with heroin by using a needle; you use a spoon first to cook it up, and then you shoot up. I was thinking how crazy and scary this was, and now I knew why a lot of our spoons disappeared from the kitchen drawer over the summer. We weren't putting the whole thing together at the time.

The next day, my sister came to visit and while we were upstairs talking, Mark went downstairs for a little bit. When he came back up, he talked with my sister, and then went upstairs to his room. My sister waited at the house with Mark while I went to pick my daughter up from school. When I pulled into my driveway, I saw a detective outside my door talking with my sister. He told me he was in our area and had witnessed Mark running out to a friend's car, then running back to our house. Because the detective knew about Mark's situation, he became suspicious, and the friend was then approached by the police who told them Mark had given him money to go and buy heroin. The detective said my sister had let him in the house to talk with Mark, and he had told Mark what he saw and said he needed to get help. When the detective left, I talked to Mark about what had just happened, and he denied everything, which was what I thought he would do.

We were out of our minds with sadness, and then I had to go to a hearing with Mark at the college, where he admitted to what had taken place. The woman in charge of the hearing said he could go to another college but would not be able to come back to this one because of their school policy. She told me that Mark handled himself in a very mature manner. We tried to see if there was any way we could persuade them to give him another chance, but she said it would not be possible. My husband and I were really hoping that maybe with going to Narcotics Anonymous meetings, getting some counseling at the college, and our continued support, Mark could work on himself and get better and be able to go back to that school. We just didn't have a clue how deep his addiction really was. The next thing to focus on was how the courts would handle the new charge.

I wished we had been able to jump on the situation before this happened, but we didn't get to him soon enough. I know I made every effort to get involved and try to fix things. I felt really sorry for him; he was my son, and he was highly addicted to drugs. It totally breaks your heart when you see what your kid used to be like and then what they became as a result of taking drugs. Drugs had taken Mark to a dark place. I was told heroin was such a bad addiction for most people. They say you only have to try it once, and you are immediately hooked. I later found out that he was doomed after he tried the drug OxyContin. I was told that once you get addicted to this, in most cases you eventually move on to using heroin.

• • •

Chapter Eighteen

We were advised by our lawyer that a court date had been set to discuss the new charge. My parents were so upset and decided it would be better if Mark kept busy for the time being, so they took him to a place near our home that they thought might be hiring, and with their help, he got the job right away.

It was time for my daughter's book fair at school which I had volunteered to help out at. I couldn't make it, so Mark offered to go in place of me. He saw a lot of his old teachers from elementary school, and he told some of them about how he was at college and had gotten a scholarship. He later told me he told them this because he didn't want them to think he was a dummy. I think he was feeling the pain of the actions that got him dismissed from college.

Mark's previous charges were juvenile charges and since probation wasn't completed yet, the new charge he picked up was considered a violation of his probation.

When it came time for court again, he was drug tested, and the judge sentenced him to the juvenile detention center for a little over a month, due to the new charge, and the next court date was tentatively scheduled. Mark would be brought back to court at that time to appear in front of the judge who would review his case.

When it was time to visit Mark at the detention center on Sundays at a certain time, my husband and I went to visit, Mark's father went to visit him, or I would go by myself. It was very strict there regarding what you could bring in to the place. Everyone was scanned every time they went in. I kept telling myself this was no place for my son. I kept thinking that my son was stuck in this place instead of being at college, where he should be. I told Mark he had been warned about what might happen if he got in trouble at college, and that he had to accept the consequences of his actions. When I first saw Mark at the detention center, he looked depressed. He was angry that he had gotten into college and then ruined it. This is how far his disease of addiction had taken him. I really did feel bad for him, and nothing seemed right anymore. I was so sad all of the time now.

We obviously could not trust Mark at home while we both worked; he would be by himself, and he was in no shape to be left alone. All I felt was anxiety at this point. I loved my son to death, and I kept thinking, "I am not losing my kid to drugs." I was afraid for him and something needed to be done, so even though I hated that he was in the detention center, he was safe and had no access to any drugs. But I kept thinking, "I want my son back."

After being in the detention center for a little over a month, Mark was brought to court, and I met him there with our lawyer. Pending the next court date, the Judge let him out on house arrest and warned Mark he was giving him a chance so he could be home with his family for the holidays and told him not to mess it all up.

The same officer from Mark's first house arrest in high school was handling Mark, and he said, "Oh no, not this kid again." The officer and I kind of both laughed because this whole thing was so crazy. Our lives had been turned upside down for the past few years already, and insanity became the norm, as strange as this sounds. I didn't know if this was going to work either, but we felt it would be better for him to be around his family now than in a detention center.

Mark had a lot of support, and when Christmas Day came around, he was with us, and it was the best time we'd had with him in a long time. Everyone was so happy to see him, and we were all together now. I wished deep down that it could always be like it was that day.

Mark was still being drug tested at probation meetings, but the fact that he was living at home again meant he had to be watched all the time when he was not working. He was still in a vulnerable state concerning drugs. We also knew that when he was alone, anyone could drop off drugs to him. That was a concern of ours, so family tried to help us out as much as they could. I went to Narcotics Anonymous meetings with Mark as much as we could, which opened up an understanding for me about what people really are going through in their fight to stay clean. What a horrible disease this was. My husband and I talked it over, and we let Mark know we would be there to help support him, and all of his family was there too. All he had to do was reach out to any of us.

Mark and his girlfriend had still been together at this point. Even though his girlfriend's parents were upset with what had happened with Mark, they really liked him and knew he was trying to work on himself, so Mark and his girlfriend continued to stay in touch. But by February, Mark and his girlfriend of a year broke up. They spent a lot of time together, but it wasn't in the cards for them, and so they ended it, but not happily. Now he was probably even more depressed.

Each time Mark worked, I had to drop him off and pick him up. He mentioned he really needed his own car, but I told him we were not ready for that right now. He had been looking in the paper and thought that if he could keep up the payments by working full-time then he could afford one on his own. We did talk about it, but I knew this was not a good idea, so I kept dodging it when he mentioned it to me.

The weeks passed by, and I noticed he was acting really strange one day. He was nodding off, his speech was slow, and when he looked at me I could tell he didn't look right. He eventually fell asleep and slept most of the day. I decided to call my sister up and told her what I had noticed and that I was suspicious that it was heroin use again. We knew he was still under the supervision of probation so she offered to help by coming over the next morning and suggested we take him to the hospital. In the meantime I had to figure out what we were going to do as I didn't know how we would get him into the car to take him to the hospital to get him checked out. I knew he would not go willingly to the hospital, but I needed to put a plan in place. After giving it some thought, I called my sister again that day telling her I would tell Mark that we were going to take him to a car dealer because I was going to buy him a car. It was the only plan that would work, and so I told him the night before that I had decided it was time to go and buy a car. He seemed pretty excited, and I felt a little guilty at this point, knowing we were not going to look at cars, but my desire to not lose him was greater than the guilt.

When I walked past his room the next morning, I noticed Mark was dosing off standing up. I knew at that moment that Mark had probably used heroin when he got up because he was totally out of it. When I asked him when he would be ready to go, he spoke very slowly and had a weak voice, and he had put on a pair of sunglasses. My sister arrived, and the plan was in place.

Mark had no idea what was going on, and when he got in my sister's car he started dosing off again. We both wanted to cry watching him but held it all in. We didn't want to waste any more time, so my sister started driving, and within a couple of minutes she turned into the parking lot of the emergency room at the nearby hospital. Mark was awake at this point, asking why we were turning into the hospital, and my sister said she had made a wrong turn and was turning around. He kept dosing off and waking up, and finally we wound up right in front of the emergency room. I got out and ran inside to ask for a nurse on duty, and I told her our situation. I was shocked to hear her say that because he was eighteen he could not be forced to come in, but she would send someone out to talk with him.

We wound up telling him where we were and that we weren't moving until he got out and walked into the emergency room. The nurse's response was not acceptable to me or my sister, even though by law they could not force him out of the car. One of the doctors came out to talk with Mark, but he would not get out of the car. I wasn't giving up on my son, not now or ever, so I decided to call the case worker who helped me to get him into the first rehab center. She was glad that I had called her first, and she told me she would be right over. Since he still had an ankle monitor on him from the house arrest, she called the local police to come help us. While we were waiting for the police to arrive, Mark said he was going to get out of the car and walk away.

A few minutes later, two officers arrived; one recognized me from things that that had happened during Mark's high school years and they ordered Mark out of the car. They told him that if he didn't get out of the car, they would pull him out themselves. All he said to them was "this sucks," and they followed him until he was in a hospital room. I was so upset this whole time but grateful that he was now going to be treated by a doctor. I thanked the officers, and they left.

Mark was being difficult with the doctor at first, but he was under the influence of drugs. We wouldn't have expected him to be anything other than angry and abusive at this point when it came to talking with the doctor, who was asking him many questions.

He was then admitted to the emergency room, and they did all kinds of tests on him. I left the room for a little bit but was called back in because Mark was asking for me. He was screaming, cursing at the doctors, and crying; it was so awful to see him this way—I can't even explain the rage he had. Finally they put an oxygen mask on him and gave him a sedative. His heart rate had dropped which the doctor suspected was due to him overdosing. My entire family and Mark's father were called. It was the most horrible thing to be in the hospital not knowing if my son was going to make it or not. My sister and I did what we thought was the right thing to do at the time. We weren't worried about him getting into trouble at the court date coming up; all we cared about was Mark, and we prayed he would get through this.

Mark was put in intensive care with a low heart rate, and all of the immediate family made it over to the hospital, including his father. We just waited for the doctor to come in and let us know how Mark was doing. They had been able to stabilize him, and we would be able to go in and see him shortly. I just lost it in the waiting room and cried and cried. I loved my son so much, and no matter what, that love would never ever change.

When Mark woke up, he started crying because he thought he was going to jail because he had violated his probation by not being drug free. We told him we just wanted him to get well and to just focus on that. A few days later, he was well enough to go home from the hospital. He looked so good it was like nothing had ever happened. I wanted to erase the memory of what had just happened, but I had to face the reality of it. We were so happy he was okay but scared about what was going to happen at court.

$\bullet\bullet\bullet$

Chapter Nineteen

It was now time for Mark to face the charge in our county for the new violation. Because it was an out-of-state charge Mark was facing, we found out we had to first appear at a court date in that state. Then our lawyer would try to coordinate how we could combine this new charge with his juvenile violation so we could settle it all in our state instead of going to two different courts.

Because of Mark's overdose and his hospital stay, my parents suggested he receive the sacrament of the anointing of the sick to help him. We asked our pastor at my Catholic church if he could do this for us, and he agreed. He knew Mark a little, as Mark had seen him in the past to do private confessions.

When it was time for the out-of-state court date from Mark's drug possession at college, we met with our lawyer, and Mark was charged with a felony. This just hurt so bad that I can't even explain it. When it was time for the court date in our state, they had Mark drug tested first, and while we were waiting for the person to bring him to take the test, he kept saying he was fine and didn't see the point of it. My lawyer reminded him that he had overdosed and had just been in the hospital. After Mark came back from doing the test, we were sitting outside the courtroom together, waiting for the judge to call Mark back in, and Mark told me he didn't want to be here anymore. I told him to stop talking like that, and I said I was not losing him to drugs, and he said "Mom, you already did." This was so significant. This made me so upset I remember crying to my lawyer when he came out of the courtroom that if the judge put him back in the detention center temporarily until a bed was open at a rehab center, I wanted Mark watched because I didn't trust him after what he had said. I think he may have said it to me so I would persuade our lawyer to work with the judge to not send him to an inpatient rehab clinic and to just go home and go back to work like he wanted. No way was this going to happen, and the lawyer and I thought our only solution was to have Mark put back in to the detention center until a bed was available at a court-ordered rehab facility. It was supposed to only be for a short time, but it turned into longer than we expected.

The detention center could only keep him for a certain number of days. There was a bed available for him at a rehab facility, and they would be interviewing him there. Unfortunately for Mark, our lawyer had to handle the out-of-state charge first before he could go to this rehab facility, if he was even accepted.

Mark was told he would be going to a holding place first, a juvenile reception and assessment center, until the charge out of state was dealt with. We were not happy about this, as it wasn't close by, and we knew nothing about this place. I was anxious to see my son there. He was able to call me, and he told me that he had offered to be the one in charge of the Laundromat there so he would be out of his room most of the day. They even had him mow the lawn outside with one of those old push mowers. I can't imagine what he was feeling when he was in there with all of those kids.

When it was time for visitation, my husband and I went. As we pulled up to this place and saw barbed wire on top of the fence, I just shook my head and wanted to cry. Anxiety was setting in, but I didn't want my son to see me upset. We had to show identification, and then we waited until a van came to bring all of the parents behind the building to the entrance. Once inside, we had to wait again for other doors to open, and then they scan you with a wand, and finally we went into a gym where all the kids come to see their family.

We were really happy to see Mark, and I gave him a really tight hug. I didn't want to look sad and get him upset, so we sat down and had a good conversation with him about how he was going to get help. He told us that someone from the security staff was talking with him and said to just consider it a bump in the road; Mark had his whole life ahead of him and a bright future if he worked on himself and really wanted that. Mark seemed to have goals of staying clean, and once he got into the rehab facility that had been brought up, he was going to make the best of it. We weren't sure what was really going to happen, but we kept our fingers crossed and hoped for the best.

I was really aggravated about how long he had to stay there, but there were no choices. The out-of-state charge was still being handled by our lawyer so Mark could go to rehab. The wait was agonizing. Each time Mark and I spoke on the phone, he would ask me if I had heard from our lawyer yet about when they were going to handle the adult charge. It really started to get me angry about how far this had gotten, and there wasn't a damn thing we could do about. I felt bad telling my son we still had to wait to hear from our lawyer. Finally, after two months of being in that center, he was driven to a state-run rehab facility an hour and a half away from us.

I was told I needed to bring a bag of his clothes and other necessary things to the rehab facility. My sister offered to come with me, and I brought my daughter along so she could visit her brother. She had been missing him too. As we pulled up, I braced myself. I took one look at the place and my heart just sank. I could not believe he was at a rehab center again. I began thinking about how much I missed him, all the fun we used to have, all the places we had taken him to in his life, and how much his family loved him and wanted to see him do well. I wished this was all just a bad dream.

The reality of it all set in when we walked in to the rehab center, and Mark came into the room. All I did was look at his face, and I knew he was so unhappy; he looked so depressed. He said he wanted to go right back to the assessment center and had already called the place, but we told him all the places would be the same, so he would have to try to embrace it. There was nothing we could do about it. We were told he would have to spend six or seven months there, depending on how well he embraced the program.

We met the staff, and they were really friendly. It made me feel more at ease when I spoke to Mark's counselor, who said Mark had to give it some time. We knew the counselor was right, and Mark was there because he had a problem. I know Mark was a little mad at me and maybe my sister, too, for taking him to the hospital, which led to him being placed in another rehab program. Without a doubt, I am sure that this hospital incident was an indication that Mark clearly needed inpatient treatment, and I wasn't about to question what we did.

The schedule for visitation was every Friday night for about two hours. We went on occasion in the beginning but wanted him to get used to the program, so we didn't go every week. When he got adjusted, we started going every other Friday, sometimes more often. He seemed to be doing well and even played on a baseball team there. He said that was his only enjoyment, getting out and playing ball. He was assigned maintenance jobs while living there, and he even became chief for a while. This meant he helped run activities and was in charge of helping the other kids in the house. He was also able to exercise like he wanted to do. He got a few privileges and only had to share a room with one other person, compared to a room full of kids. There were times when he would call and ask me when he was getting out because he missed being home and had so many regrets about not being at college anymore. That hurt a lot, but again, what were we to do? He broke the law, and this is what happens.

While visiting Mark one time, he gave us an inventory he wrote while in the assessment center. Here is what he wrote, in his own words.

Mark's Inventory

My addiction has taken me to places I never wanted to be or thought I would be. The addiction that has been a part of me the past three years has caused major problems in my life. It has brought me guilt, shame, remorse, anger, depression, frustration, failure, denial, and disgust. It has not brought me anything good. My addiction has only kept me along the path of self-destruction. The insanity that came along with my disease is unthinkable. I was the one doing all of this, and I still cannot believe some of the insanity that was following me around. I disappointed my family, friends, and acquaintances, but most importantly, myself and God. My family does not trust me because of what I have done. I have been so fortunate to get the breaks I have gotten, and I still managed to fuck them all up. Although my life has not been the best lately, I am happy and grateful to be alive today. As I sit here and write this inventory, I feel angry, depressed, and frustrated over all of the things in my life I have missed out on because of my addiction: all of the friends I've lost, all of the extracurricular activities I gave up, quitting baseball, the summer times I've missed, the scholarship and college experience I lost out on. The thing that gets me most about that list is that I can never get them back. I've cheated, stolen, manipulated people, and used people during my active addiction, and it hurts. That is not the kind of person I am. I am a good person who cares about others. I give to others and I treat people with respect. I am religious and love God.

My addiction turned me into a different person. I cheated on the first girl I really loved. I gave up my fucking scholarship and a chance at a prestigious college. I hurt my family and friends over and over. It was selfish of me to think I was only hurting myself. It is a chain reaction, and my problems have hurt myself the most but also the people who care about me. It kills me inside to know that I made Kasey, my mom, and so many of my friends and family members cry over what I was doing to myself. I basically had it all. I had a beautiful family who supported me all the time, a scholarship to college, a nice car, perfect health, and a trusting and caring God to talk to whenever I needed him, and I still fucked everything up for myself—true insanity.

Fuck drugs and fuck addiction. I wake up in this fucking jail cell every morning and feel like shit. My skin feels dirty, and I feel like a complete failure. I look out the window at the beautiful grass and sun and feel depressed. I am bothered by the fact that my addiction has taken me this far. It must die. I want the ghost out of the closet, and I want my normal life back. As I stress over the shame and guilt that this has all brought me, I try to turn my mind to the positive points. I have a lot of positive things to look forward to in my future. I am going to stay clean and become more of an open and honest person. That is the only way I can beat it. I must accept all of this for what it is and learn from it so I never make the mistake again. I am young, and I still have my beautiful mind intact. I thank God every day for what I have and for the strength he gives me. I am going to rebuild broken relationships with friends and regain the trust of my family. As long as I keep the faith and care for others, I will make it wherever I want in life. It all starts with staying clean and keeping God by my side. All I have to do is stay clean, and I can have the satisfying and beautiful life that I want. God will always be with me.

So this is where Mark's addiction had taken him, to a very dark place. You feel so helpless as a parent when your child is going through something like this. I really believe heroin is the devil. A family member compared it to a boa constrictor that squeezes the life out of our kids. Anyone can challenge me on this, but I believe marijuana is the gateway drug to addiction because I witnessed it firsthand with my son. I know that not everyone becomes addicted, but everyone is changed by using the drug. No one knows before their first time if they will become an addict. The future is always unwritten. It's like trying anything; before you try it, how do you know how it will affect you? But once you try it, it's too late to take it back. I know that if Mark had known what was behind that door, he would not have opened it.

A TV movie from the 1970s, *The Boy in the Plastic Bubble*, in many ways reminded me of Mark's addiction. In the movie, John Travolta plays a young man who, because of an immunity disorder, could not venture outside of his sterile plastic bubble home, or he would risk fatal illness; therefore, the plastic bubble was a place of safety for him. I wish I could have put Mark in a plastic bubble where he would have been safe. However, an addict cannot live in a plastic bubble; they have to venture out into the world with all its temptations at some point.

Chapter Twenty

As time went on, Mark was embracing the program they had there and doing extremely well. There was nothing we could do for him except wait until the rehab facility said he was ready to leave. He did prove himself in that place. When some of my family came along with us one time for a family dinner, Mark was chosen as one of the speakers. We were all amazed at what he said, and just by hearing him give that speech, we had every confidence that he was going to complete the program and stay sober once he was out. He had many goals he wanted to achieve for his future.

College was one of the items on his list of things to get back into. One day the rehab facility had a man come in from a college up north that had what they called a recovery dorm. He was the director of the program at the dorm, and he had been asked to speak to the kids about this college. It was about maintaining a sober life by attending addict meetings and following the twelve-step recovery program while attending college on campus. There would be nothing outside these dorms saying "this is where recovering addicts stay." Only the person staying in the dorm would know. Mark had mentioned that he toured a college near the rehab facility he was staying at but was interested in this recovery dorm at this college up north. It sounded really good to us, and we made a plan that we would visit this college when Mark was discharged.

It was now the end of November, and I phoned our lawyer to let him know that with the approval of Mark's counselor, we were ready for him to set up a court date for Mark's release from rehab. Mark had been doing amazingly well; he had been very respectful while in the rehab center, and the counselors there said he was a really good kid and was embracing the program. Mark's main counselor said he will do very well in life as long as he thinks first and remembers what the consequences would be in future situations that concerned drugs.

A date was set up, and we thought he would be coming home that day after court, but that was not the case. Everything got so mixed up with the courts, and when we met at the courthouse, there was no work written up for his release; I think there was just a miscommunication. I flipped out on our lawyer and asked why Mark wasn't being released that day and why we had to wait two more weeks. I was so upset and angry that I had taken a day off from work to come to court and wasn't bringing my son home.

After court was rescheduled, we again had to say our good-byes to each other, and Mark was taken back to the rehab facility very depressed. He had even brought all of his things because he was so sure he would not have to go back. This was a really bad day, and I think I cried most of the way home. While driving home, I started thinking about all the things that had happened. How could this have happened? How come there was no control? Why did my son have to have an addiction? How come he couldn't just listen to us? Why did he keep on going? How could an addiction to drugs take him this far? No one has the true answer as to why things happen the way they do. I still could not believe our lives were all about coping with addiction, arrests, probation, counseling galore, inpatient rehab, outpatient rehab, twelve-step meetings, and many hearings. It took a lot of sacrifice to handle everything that we had to in order to help Mark, and that is what you do when you love your child. Your child's problem becomes your problem too. You don't turn your back on your child and look the other way.

The next two weeks seemed like the longest weeks of my life. The day before court, Mark's father picked him up and brought him back to his house until Mark got the call that he had to report to the probation department in the afternoon. I was really upset, because I thought I was going to see him that day, but we spoke on the phone and he told me that he was being put in a shelter overnight instead of coming home that night. That was the ruling by the courts and then the next day it was time. I finally arrived at court and met up with Mark. We were so happy to see each other. His father had come too but could not stay for long, and our court session had been delayed. Finally, it was our turn, and we were called in to the courtroom.

The judge talked to Mark a little bit and asked me if I wanted to say something. I told the judge I was really confident that Mark had progressed really well at the rehab facility. I told him that at first I wasn't sure about the place he was put into, but after visiting every other week or more, I got to know the counselors there and how the program was run, and I was happy Mark had gotten used to being there and was, most importantly, working on himself.

The prosecutor of course was not convinced enough time had been spent there, which was seven months by then. Mark had also been at the assessment center for two months, which was a complete waste of time, and before that he was at the detention center. It had been nine months since Mark had been home. Our lawyer discussed the recovery dorm at the college and said that in order to get into this college, he needed to act quickly to ensure a January enrollment. This would mean he would be living up there, about one and half hours away from us. We felt maybe this was the best thing for him right now, due to all of the bad influences in the area.

The judge wasn't too convinced at first, but our lawyer mentioned that he had done exceptionally well at the rehab facility, and the counselors really liked him and said he had done really well in the program. They were happy with the progress that Mark had made there. The judge then made the decision for his release and for Mark to be on probation for about a year. A fine was to be paid for the latest out-of-state charge he had. He still had to report to probation, and as far as the college went, they would take care of everything up there when he would get to the college, such as making sure Mark would be attending twelve-step meetings. There was also a counselor on the campus he planned to see.

When we left court, I think we were just so happy Mark was coming home. Mark kept talking about all the positive things he would concentrate on when he got home. We were told to call a place near our house where they had individual counseling for the time being, and we found out where all the Narcotics Anonymous meetings were in our town. I made the call for the counseling, but you had to wait until there was availability, so I started taking him to meetings in the meantime to help him stay on the straight path.

Mark had originally brought up that there was a half-way house not far from us where he could live when he got out of the rehab. He could work and go to school, and he would be around people all the time who were also recovering from addictions. It was suggested by the rehab center he had been in, but I was upset at the thought of him living in a place like this because we had hopes of him going to another college since he had done so well in the rehab program. I also knew that it would mean he would be on a strict schedule, and we would not be seeing him much. I had really missed him so much while he was away. I also felt we needed to build on our relationship since he was away for so long. My daughter hadn't really seen him much for almost a year, and I wanted them to be together as much as possible too. If he was at college, he could still come home and visit whenever he wanted to. He decided to look into the halfway house just in case he changed his mind.

Mark finally made contact with the director of the recovery program at the college, and my husband and I took a drive up with Mark to see it. The director showed us the campus, and it looked nice to all three of us. We really wanted to see what it would have looked like during the day when classes were in session, but we toured it during the holidays, so that was not possible. After the tour, Mark said if he got accepted, he would like to go there, and so we waited for the response from the college. Not too long after applying, Mark received word that he was accepted, and we were so happy for him.

Twenty-One

It was a week before Christmas, and a welcome home party for Mark was planned. It turned out to be a great day, and the family was so happy to see him. Since everything was going really well, I decided it was time to take him to look at cars. We knew he was going to need one since this college was far away. We were told that he could work something out with administration to have a car on campus because some of the twelve-step meetings he would be going to were off campus.

Mark's welcome home party, December 2009

• • •

One night I took him to test drive some cars, and we spotted a beautiful, white Pontiac G6, and that was the car he really wanted. I decided to buy it but told him we had to hold off a little bit before we could. I planned to surprise him Christmas morning with it. His license would not be reinstated until three days after Christmas. He was so excited to drive and because he had been away and had done so well, we trusted him more. Everyone was so relieved that he was going to be getting on with his life now. If he ever needed anyone's help with anything, he knew he could count on us or anyone in the family.

Two days before Christmas, I went and picked up the car and asked the guy who owned a gas station across from us if I could park it out of sight for the two days until early Christmas morning. When the morning arrived, I went and picked up the car and pulled it into our driveway. It was Mark's last gift that we gave him, and he was totally surprised to get it that day. That is all I needed to see, a smile on my son's face when he got in his car. It was a great day for all of us.

Before college started in January, Mark had to attend an orientation day because now he was considered a transfer student since he had already attended another college. It was an all-day thing, and I let him take his car up. When we finally spoke, he said he had to take a written test while up there and missed some of the orientation going on, but overall, it was a really good day. When he got home, I could tell something good was up because he had a big smile on his face and told me he had even met a girl at orientation and got her number. I told him I was happy for him and that things were going to turn around for him now.

A couple of weeks later, it was time for Mark to start college. My husband really wanted to go but couldn't that day, and so Mark's father, my sister, and I went up to the new dorm to help Mark move in. We were really excited for Mark to get a fresh new start in a new area. I was hoping that he would like it up there and that he had plans to get involved in the school. When we were done, it was hard to say good-bye because I felt we did not have enough time together after he got out of rehab, but I knew that he had to get on with his life now. At this point I had to let go of whatever I was feeling now that he would be on his own again, but it put my mind at ease knowing that he was going to get counseling on campus and that he would be going to regular meetings.

After a week of being at the college, Mark called to tell me he really liked some of his classes but as far as this college went, it was a suitcase college, meaning that there were a lot more people that commuted than who stayed in a dorm, and most people went home on the weekends. He said when he went to work out at the gym, no one was there, and it wasn't what he had thought it would be. It was nothing like the other college, but I told him he had to give it a chance, and that he hadn't been there that long. He did not have his car on campus yet, but he asked me if he could have it, as he would need it to get to the meetings off campus now and could not rely on other people to bring him. I decided to let him have it, and on the next weekend he came home, he took it back to school. He had also applied for a job that would be off campus and would require a car also.

One weekend while he was up at college, Mark mentioned that he had received a flyer about a skiing trip up the mountains, and he wanted to go. He told me a lot of people were planning on going, and the girl he had just met was also going. If he went on the trip, he was to leave the next weekend on Saturday and would be back at the school by Sunday night. He said the name of the resort really fast, and I had never heard of it, but there were many places to stay up there. Not putting too much thought into it and glad that he was interested in going, I told him to bring the flyer home so I could see it. I knew I didn't need to give him the money because he already had it in his account. He planned on coming home for a little bit the day before the trip so he could get his skiing things. Friday arrived and Mark came home and showed me the flyer. I told him it looked like it would be a fun trip and glad he was going. He got his things together and soon headed back up to college.

I told Mark to give me a call whenever he could to let me know how it was. The next day I decided to go to the gym. As I was heading in, I got a call from one of my brothers. We talked for a little bit, and I told him that Mark was on a big skiing trip with his school. My brother said, "I just had a talk with Mark just a little while ago and he never mentioned any skiing trip." "I talked with him for over an hour too." I said, "I talked to him just before he said he was leaving for the trip." "That is strange that you didn't talk about this." My brother said, "I will check the time on my cell that Mark called me and I will ring you back." After my brother called me right back with the time, I just knew Mark was lying to me because he told my brother he was going to be getting ready soon to go out with friends. I was really agitated at this point and disappointed that he had to make up going on a trip. He didn't have to go on the trip if he didn't want to; it was up to him. I had never met the girl, as he had just started seeing her, and I did not have her number, so I couldn't find anything out. Now I was thinking, "Why did he have to make up this story that he was going on a skiing trip?"

I decided not to call Mark, so I waited until he called me the next day to see what he had to say. I told my brother not to call him again either because then Mark would know that I knew he wasn't telling me the truth. The next day was Sunday, and Mark finally called. I asked him if he was having a good time there, and he said he was getting ready to go skiing again before they headed home, and he would call me later. Later that day I couldn't take it anymore, and I called him back. He answered, and I asked him why he hadn't told his uncle about the ski trip. Mark insisted he was on the bus on his way home and he had gone on the trip. I think he could tell that I knew he was lying, so he said he had to go and that he would call me when he got back to school. I was pretty sure he did not go on the trip, but when he called me, I did not fight with him over the phone because he started to bring up the trust issue again, and I had had enough.

Now I know that Mark was back to being addicted to drugs by then, and when you are on drugs, you don't think rationally. We really believed he went on that trip, and he talked to my parents after the weekend, saying he had a great time and even went ice fishing. I had not told my parents yet about the phone call with my brother, and when they mentioned the ice fishing to me, I actually had to laugh at that. I was wondering where he could have gone for the weekend, and then began to be upset. I was hoping that he hadn't fallen back into the same type of people he used to hang out with in high school who were doing drugs, but it seemed like it could be a possibility.

His counseling on the campus was just getting set up. It should have started immediately when he got on that campus, but that's not the way it works. Things get delayed when people are trying to get the help that they need, and that is where they fall through the cracks. I had seen it before when we were getting him help during his high school years.

I don't think it would have mattered whether he went away to college or if he had lived at home and gone to a community college, because addiction is addiction, and you can't escape it. He was at a point where he just couldn't help himself—the addiction was too great—and I'm sure the strong cravings were there. At this point I really didn't know what to do.

He was already talking about switching to another college after the year was up. He had been talking to one of his teachers and confided in him about where he used to go to college. The teacher wanted to see a transcript of his grades, and when he did, he said he would have no problem getting in somewhere else.

I told him that he had to give this college a chance first; he was lucky he was even at a college, but we would support him if he still wasn't happy by the end of the year. His teacher said to keep up his grades for the rest of the year, and if by the end of the year he still didn't like it, then he could probably transfer out.

Twenty Two

The weekend was approaching, and Mark said he was coming home on Friday and would be giving the girl he was dating a ride home, and then he would be home. The day before Mark was to come home, I had a lot going on with work and running around doing errands later on in the evening. I was out with my daughter, and when we came back, to my surprise, I saw Mark's car in the driveway. When I walked in, he was talking with my husband, and we gave each other a hug, but I noticed he wasn't how he usually had been when we saw each other recently, full of life. He said he wanted to surprise us, so he came home a day early; he didn't have any classes on Friday anyway. He said, "I just dropped off the girl I'm seeing, and I can't wait for you to meet her." "You are really going to like her." I said, "I hope we meet her soon and you can have her over whenever you want to."

Valentine's Day was coming up on Sunday, and a friend of Mark's from another college was having people over.

Mark and some other people were planning on going out to his friend's college on Saturday, so there were already some plans made for the weekend. My daughter, Karla, had school on Friday, and there was going to be a delayed opening due to the weather. Not knowing that Mark was going to arrive a day early, I had made plans to drop her off at my friend's house whose daughter went to the same school, and he was going to take them to school to help me out. I changed the plans because Mark offered to take Karla to school the next morning, and she wanted him to take her, so I agreed.

I was with both of them for a little while, and I decided to ask Mark why he was not acting the way he usually did with me when we saw each other. I told him that for someone who was surprising us, he really didn't seem that happy when Karla and I walked in the door. He told me that he got what I was saying, and I told him to stand up, and we gave each other the tightest hug ever. I told him that this was how I wanted him to be the next time he walked through our door.

After our talk, Mark and Karla were hanging out together, and when I asked her to get ready for bed, Karla kept asking me if she could stay up a little longer so she could be with her brother, and I gave in every time because they were having such a great time. I know she had really been missing him.

When it was too late for them to stay up later, they both came up to my room. I remember telling them how happy I was having them both together. I brought up that Valentine's Day was coming up, and they would be getting presents then. Before Karla went to bed, Mark told her to wake him up at 8:30 a.m., and he would get ready and drop her off at school.

After Karla went to sleep, I gave Mark his card early and told him to keep it in his room, but he couldn't open it until Valentine's Day. We had put a note in his card saying he was going to get some baseball tickets, and he could pick the games he wanted to go to. I told him I loved him very much, and I hoped everything was getting better for him.

After talking with me for a little bit, Mark said he was going to watch a little TV. We hugged each other, and I told him that I loved him, like I always do; he told me he loved me also then went into his room.

When I had gotten up during the night, I walked past his door; I could see under the door that the light was on and could hear that the TV was on. This was nothing out of the ordinary, as a lot of times he would fall asleep with the TV on and sometimes with the light on also. I tried to open the door so I could shut off the TV and turn off his light, but it was locked so I let it go.

The next morning I had to be at work by 9:00 a.m., and I had to pick up something I had ordered at my friend's house before heading into work. Before leaving I walked by Mark's room and checked to see if his door was unlocked yet, but it wasn't. Thinking nothing of it, I left a little before 8:30 a.m. and woke my daughter up as I was leaving. I then left, went to my friend's house to pick up what I had ordered, stopped at a local convenience store, and as soon as I got into my car to head into work, I got a call from my daughter. She said Mark wasn't moving. I asked her what she meant and told her to just push him a little to wake him up. Then she said when she tried to open his door to wake him up, it was locked. She remembered that her friend had taught her how to use a hair clip to unlock a door, so she got one and played with the knob until it opened. I asked her if he was in his bed, and she said he was lying on the floor on his side. My heart was racing, and she was crying. I told her to stay put, and I raced home. While driving home, I called my husband, told him what Karla had said, and asked him to meet me at the house as soon as possible.

I flew through the door. Karla was downstairs waiting for me, and I ran up to Mark's room. I was really distraught when I saw him; he wasn't moving, and my daughter started crying again. I picked up the phone and dialed 911. I told the operator right away that my daughter had found my son, and when the operator asked if I knew CPR, I was really emotional and told her I did not think he was alive, and I began screaming, asking where the ambulance was. Right after I said this, a cop was at my door. He went up to Mark's room and told us we had to go downstairs. It was only a matter of minutes before a detective also came in, and I heard the ambulance too. The medical examiner arrived, and after I heard the cop calling off the ambulance, I knew my beautiful son had passed away. He was only nineteen years old. I know that I was in shock mode at this point and was totally numb.

While waiting downstairs, I called the pastor of my church, crying, and asked him if he could come over to say a prayer. While waiting for the pastor to come, I called my parents, and as soon as my dad picked up the phone, I told him what had happened. He screamed and could not believe it and told me he would wait for my mom to get home, and they would call back. Then I called one of my sisters at work. When I finally got through to her, she screamed and cried, and they had to take her into a room to calm her down. My parents got in touch with the rest of my siblings. I had also called Mark's father, and he was on his way over with his wife. My husband got in contact with his own parents too.

Everything happened so fast, and I think everyone was in complete shock. When the toxicology test was done to determine what drugs were found in his system, we found out it was a combination of ecstasy and heroin. This gave me such a sick feeling.

Any parent that has lost a child will tell you that unless you experience it, you really have no clue as to what it is like. There is nothing worse. All of your hopes and dreams for your child are shattered. How do you ever get over this? You don't. It stays with you for the rest of your life.

When I look back on this now, I know there was nothing more we could have done for my son. Heroin had him, and there was no turning back. It was a strong addiction that was very difficult to control. I know he tried to fight it but was in too deep. I will forever remember Mark telling me he was going to walk away when he was first introduced to drugs, but he gave in to the peer pressure. As a result of that decision, he had a life of continual misery. His life spiraled out of control for about five years because of his addiction to drugs. Any parent who says their kids are too smart and would never fall into the temptation had better think again, because it doesn't matter how smart your child is or how involved they are in school. It can happen to anyone's child, just like it happened to my Mark. He was a very smart kid who excelled in school. He was involved in sports growing up but lost interest in everything when he was on drugs. The addiction destroyed his whole life.

It makes me sad to think that we could not stop Mark's addiction. Nothing could be worse than doing everything you possibly can to help your child and having it backfire on you. Drugs really change you as a person. I saw the change in my son's personality when he became someone that was not his true character. He was the type of kid who had enormous potential. He didn't wake up one day and say, "Hey, I think I want to become a drug addict today." It was the gradual disease of drug addiction that led him down this horrible path. We spent five years of continually trying to get him well. Without a doubt, I know that if I hadn't involved the police, my son would have died sooner.

I used to say, "Why, God, why? Why *my* son?" But I was told we are not to question it. As I was watching Mark suffer, I began to understand. Not too long after Mark had passed away, my daughter and I were talking about everything that had happened. She knew exactly what happened. She said something one night before going to bed. It really got to me, and I will never forget it. I was telling her how much I missed her brother, and she said, "Mom, Mark is so lucky. He gets to meet God first." I gave her a big hug and was totally blown away by this, and I began to think how beautiful it was that she would even think to say this at only eleven years of age.

Seeing kids who are Mark's age is a constant reminder of what I lost. It is a tremendous void in my life I can't even explain. I miss our talks and all of the good times we had and places we went together; I miss his sense of humor, all the hugs he gave me, and his sensitivity. Our family will never forget this special kid—he will be forever missed. I know our lives will never be the same now that he's not with us. He was my beautiful son and a loving brother, grandson, nephew, cousin, and friend.

I know that there was nothing left unsaid with my son. He knew that I loved him and was there for him, and I am at peace with that. I believe he struggled so hard but he could not overcome his addictions, and I believe God relieved him of his struggles. Because of my strong faith, I know that God did not take my son. God saved my son.

When I look back on the night before my son passed away, neither of us knew it, but we were both saying good-bye when we gave each other that tight hug. Because of everything that has happened, I know I will never take life for granted.

No one ever knows when it is their time to go, but when my time is up, I will go to my grave knowing that I did everything I possibly could have done to save my son's life.

Made in the USA
Middletown, DE
30 January 2018